Under the Shadow of the Hill

MONTACUTE
1939 – 1945

CLARENCE BRADLEY

ryelands

First published in Great Britain in 2015
Copyright © Clarence Bradley 2015

Disclaimer.
The author has used information given to him, in good faith.
Should this prove to be inaccurate, the material will be
corrected in future editions

A CIP record for this title is available from the British Library

ISBN 978 1 906551 39 1

RYELANDS
Halsgrove House,
Ryelands Business Park,
Bagley Road, Wellington, Somerset TA21 9PZ
Tel: 01823 653777   Fax: 01823 216796
email: sales@halsgrove.com

Part of the Halsgrove group of companies.
Information on all Halsgrove titles is available at: www.halsgrove.com

Printed in China by Everbest Printing Co Ltd

Contents

Acknowledgements

I would like to thank everyone who kindly told me their stories and trusted me with their precious documents and photographs. Without their help, this book would not have been written and all would have been forgotten:

Brendon Owen, Janet Jenkins, Somerset Heritage Centre, Jack Sweet, The National Trust, Vincent and Beryl Baker, Montacute Baptist Church, Margaret Bussell, Charlie Northam, Julian Geard, Marilyn Marsh, Peggy Gaylard, Phyllis Tresidder, Jacqueline Fox, Joyce Monaghan, Ray Bartlett, Keith Hann, Sarah Dike, Norman Tulett, Amy Yates, Stanley Stagg, Bill Fall, Ken Trotman, Jo and David Morgan, Major Warrick, Bob Fenning, Mary Purdy, John Dunston, Humphrey Hamlin, Vi Myram, Bill Inglett, Norman Pilton, Amy Bugler, Shirley Ware, Chris Brimble, Carol Roberts née Brimble, Doug Carswell, Rosie & Terry Jones, Yeovil Library, St Catherine's church.

I am very grateful to Mr Andrew Keasler of the Defence Attaché Office of the Embassy of the United States of America for the help he has given me.

My grateful thanks to Angie Hodges and Beryl Baker for typing and structuring my book. Also to Vincent Baker, Chairman of Montacute Parish Council, for his assistance.

To Philip Hodges aFIAP, cPAGB, for the photography, front and back cover design, and preparation for submission to the publishers.

And to all the many other contributors too numerous to list.

The Author dedicates this book to the People of Montacute.

Montacute

The village of Montacute, Somerset, lies 4 miles west of Yeovil, 22 miles east of Taunton and 40 miles from Bristol to the north. It is shielded to the south by woodland and St Michael's Hill to the west. It currently has a population of around 830.

Its main attraction is the National Trust property of Montacute House, built between 1588-1601. It was the residence of the Phelips family and was taken over by the National Trust in 1931. The parish church is St Catherine's, with its tall magnificent tower. The village also has a Baptist church built in hamstone with a unique outside staircase which accesses the gallery to accommodate larger congregations.

The houses and buildings have mostly been built with hamstone, a soft mellow stone which was excavated in the local quarry on Ham Hill, still worked by the family firm of Harvey Stone.

The Saxon name for Montacute was Leodgaresburg and the ruling Lord was Tofig, King Cnut's Standard Bearer.

The legend of St Michael's Hill was that a black flint cross was dug out of the hill and taken to Waltham Abbey, Essex.

When the Normans arrived, the name of the village was changed to Montacute – Mons Acutus – the pointed hill. The Earl of Mortain, King William's half brother, was responsible for this part of the shire and would have fortified the hill with a wooden keep, and a surrounding bailey made of timber. Of the castle or keep there are no remains but in its place was built a folly dated 1760 which is accessible and gives a panoramic view of the surrounding countryside.

The Priory, otherwise known as the Abbey Gatehouse, announced the entrance to the now extinct Abbey. The Abbey would have been inhabited by Cluniac monks from France who wore the black habit. The Abbey was destroyed during the Reformation by Henry VIII. The gatehouse is now a farmhouse and still lived in by Mrs Jenkins and family.

Montacute still has a village school which is very important. Its catchment area includes the neighbouring village of Odcombe and the school's name is All Saints.

The original school which lies opposite the church was built in 1847 with a further addition in 1895. Many village children of earlier generations were taught there and, like many Victorian schools, it was later sold and turned into a private house.

The village has two hostelries, the "King's Arms" and the "Phelips' Arms", which are still being supported by the village residents. Sadly, the Working Men's Club, built in 1892, has now closed after serving the community from 1928 to 2013.

Montacute has endured its share of trouble and upsets over the years. One particular incident which took place between 1833 and 1838, was a feud between the Reverend Albion Cox and the bell ringers.

During that period many villages had their own society or club to help people who were sick in their old age. Montacute's Club Day was the first Sunday after Trinity.

It was a tradition for the bells to be rung to celebrate the club day but the vicar forbade the bells to be rung. This upset the members and parish-ioners. The ringers decided to continue ringing the bells but the vicar cut the bell ropes so the bells could not be rung. The members and the parish-ioners picketed the church in protest. The Magistrates were informed and on hearing this the protesters took refuge in the surrounding countryside. The local Yeomanry, under Captain Quantock, hunted the men down and they were sentenced to six months in Ilchester jail

War took its toll in later years with the First World War when 13 men from Montacute were killed in action serving their country. Their names are inscribed with honour on the War Memorial inside Montacute church together with the names of five men from the Second World War.

It is these men and women who served their country whom people should honour with their gratitude. They laid down their lives for the cause of freedom.

Once again, in 1938, Montacute was preparing for war. A letter was received by the Parish Council recommending air raid precautions be taken, so a meeting was held and Captain C. A. Hayes was nominated to organise the A.R.P. Approximately 30 parishioners attended. Captain Hayes gave a long and detailed statement of the measures required.

War Memorial inside St Catherine's church, Montacute.

War was declared on 3 September 1939 and the people of Montacute, with other villages, towns and cities, prepared themselves to be alert and watchful.

With German armies invading Holland, Denmark, Norway and throughout Europe and eventually the fall of France, the Battle for Britain was about to begin. The British war machine came into being and, with Winston Churchill's invigorating speeches, people rallied and prepared themselves for what was to come.

A siren was obtained and installed at Montacute House.

A St John's nursing unit was created and manned by local people and based at Abbey Farm.

St John's nurses at Abbey Farm. Back row left to right: *Pat Ewens, Chris Lawrence, Mrs Cannon, Mrs Little, Mr Cole, Miss Farthing, Grace Welch, Mary Diamond, Mary Knight.* Middle row left to right: *Clara Drayton, Flo Drayton, Connie Scammel, Mrs Ewens, Miss Hodder, Miss Farthing, Mrs Pilton.* Front row left to right: *Jean Dunston, Sylvia King, Nancy Cole, Betty Gaylard, Jean Syms, Sylvia Cole, Joy Bowden.*

The wartime Constabulary of the village, also photographed outside Abbey Farm. Back row left to right: *Ralph Gaylard, Bert Rowles, Hugh Cannon, not known, Rex Drayton.* Bottom row: *have yet to be identified by the author.*

In March 1940 the Yeovil District Council offered to supply Montacute with a fire pump and equipment and asked for volunteers to be trained to use it. A draft scheme was suggested for fire watch duties.

The parish was to be split into four crews, and for A.R.P. purposes, each area was to have approximately twenty volunteers to take a night each in turn. Taunton & Thorne Factory had regular fire watches and also had a system installed to warn residents of the parish of the danger of fire and bombings. Particular vigilance was needed for incendiary bombs as these could cause immediate fires on roofs and properties and the A.R.P. was in place to alleviate the problem.

In 1940 large numbers of military personnel were billeted in the village with the soldiers sharing people's homes and military vehicles using the roads and Montacute House Park.

The Chairman of the Parish Council received a request from the Officer in Command of military personnel stationed here to give permission for the troops to use the football pitch. The request was approved provided the O.C. got in touch with the Secretary of the Football Club.

On 17 April 1940, it was reported that an army lorry had damaged the fountain in the Borough. The Chairman of the Parish Council and the Clerk interviewed the Commanding Officer and he paid 15 shillings to get the joints repaired. It was agreed to ask Mr A. Shoemark to do the necessary repair work.

At around the same time, an army lorry of 225 or 226 Battery knocked down a gas lamp on the corner of the Borough. Southern Command admitted liability and paid £3 towards the repair of the damage to the lamp standard.

It was decided to remove all the mantles from the public gas lamps to sustain blackout rules and for additional safety Mr Rogers was asked to paint the constriction stone in Wash Lane white.

In August 1940 a circular letter was received by the Parish Council regarding the prevention of enemy aircraft landing in neighbouring fields and it was requested that obstacles be put in place to prevent this. (It is most likely to have been in respect of gliders not powered aircraft.) The fields most likely to have been affected would have been the warren on Ham Hill Road or the fields near the railway station. It was decided nothing could be done by the Parish Council.

A letter of application was received from Stoke sub Hamdon Flight of

1032 Squadron Air Training Corps for permission to use the football pitch. After a discussion it was decided all players would contribute 3d each with a minimum total of 2s.9p per match. (I was a member of the same squadron in later years at Martock – Author.)

During the heavy bombing of London, Montacute began to receive a number of evacuees to be billeted in the village and this was widespread in other local communities. The vicar of Montacute, Reverend Beechey, and Mrs Keep of the Old Vicarage opposite the church, acted as Evacuation Officers.

The evacuees arrived at Yeovil Town Station and boarded buses to be taken to Montacute parish church. There was plenty of bustling around as you can imagine, but every child was allotted a billet with a family in the village.

As the war progressed, a further request was made to the village to take more evacuees but it was felt unsuitable as being too close to Westland's airfield in the event of a bombing attack on the airfield and Yeovil.

Montacute Baptist church.

Most residents and parishioners in the village grew their own vegetables to compensate for rationing. A lot of people also kept chickens for eggs and cockerels were fattened to eat. Some families kept a couple of pigs for food – meat and sausages and also used the offal.

Concern was raised in Montacute for the safety of the children attending school in both Montacute and Stoke in the event of an air attack. The Parish Council protested at the inadequacy of shelters. A letter was sent to Mr Richards J.P. at Stoke to ask him to add his support in this matter.

MONTACUTE BAPTIST CHURCH MINUTE BOOK 1939
October 15 1939

After the afternoon service Mr Osborne reported to the church that the Manse had been commandeered by the Southern Command for quartering troops and emphasised the difficulty of lodging any objections. It was agreed to accept this under the exceptional circumstances prevailing.

Mr Osborne also confirmed that the Rev. A. W. Gummer-Butt would, contrary to expectations, be able to commence his pastorate here on 5 November and that all the necessary arrangements were in hand.

December 13 1939

Mr Osborne reported on the military occupation of church property and confirmed that the way in which the military were conducting this occupation was far from satisfactory.

May 19 1940

In spite of the severe handicap due to uncertain conditions and the shortage of premises owing to military occupation the services were encouraging and well attended.

September 30 1940

The Harvest Thanksgiving service conducted by Rev. A. D. Fraser of Yeovil was well attended and the church tastefully decorated. The harvest sale of produce was held on 1 October. Due to the military occupation of the school room, the vicar kindly allowed this to be held in the C. of E. school. Mr W. A. Drayton was auctioneer.

September 3 1941

The Chairman mentioned at a meeting that there were about 20 or so young men who had been connected with the church in HM Forces and suggested that a list should be made containing all these names and that the names should be read out before prayers on the first Sunday of each month. Mrs Hockey was appointed to the task. (Pages 13/14)

October 19 1941

A church meeting was held when Mr Osborne reported that the Yeovil RDC had stated that they were about to requisition all unnecessary iron railings for the Government. It was decided that a letter be sent to the Clerk of the RDC objecting to the requisitioning of the railings in front of the chapel.

April 26 1942
A united service was held in the parish church in connection with the National Aid to Russia Week. The service was led by Rev. R. T. Beechey. There was a large congregation including the Home Guard and Civil Services. Collection amounted to £9.18s.6d.

July 1 1942
Mr R. L. Gaylard reported that he had heard of the death of Mr C. W. Dare of Henley Manor, Crewkerne (late of Abbey Farm, Montacute) and proposed that a letter of sympathy be sent to Mrs Dare and family.

Mr Dare had been closely associated with the chapel during the time he resided at Abbey Farm from 1915-1925 when he was Deacon and Treasurer.

September 1 1943
It was decided to open a service fund to send cigarettes to the men now in HM Forces who had been connected with the church and Sunday School.

September 6 1943
It was decided to continue afternoon services for the time being, the possibility of one evening service to be considered later in the event of a reduction of blackout regulations being announced.

November 24 1943
It was reported that £4.11s.0d had been collected for the service fund and that 11 members serving overseas had each been sent 150 cigarettes. To those serving in the Home Guard it was decided to send a greetings card and 2s.6d each.

October 25 1944
Mr Osborne received a letter from Mrs Wilton to inform the church of the loss of her only son Reginald Wilton killed on active service in France.

October 16 1945
Mr Osborne reported that the compensation for the Manse from the Military

Land Agent had been received. The final figure agreed on was £19.18s.10d. less £3 for electric light installation, the original claim being for £144.4s.6d.

November 28 1945

Mr Osborne stated that a claim for dilapidation in connection with the School Hall and premises amounting to £151.7s.0d. had been forwarded to the Military Land Agent.

December 13 1945

Mr Osborne introduced the "Victory Thanksgiving Fund" which raised £150 for reconstruction at home, and on the continent. It was decided to defer the allocation of these funds until the New Year.

January 19 1946

The School Hall was used for the first time since it was requisitioned, in 1939, by the military.

Note... During the Americans' use of the church some redecoration (painting) took place but the soldiers were not very good at decorating and some of their handywork is still visible today...

Green paint wasted at the top of the flight of stairs in the Baptist church.

NAMES ON MONTACUTE ROLL OF HONOUR
FROM THE BAPTIST CHURCH

HORACE BRAKE	R.A.F.
IVOR BRAKE	
NORMAN BURFIELD	SOM. L.I. WOUNDED IN ACTION
KENNETH BUSSELL	ROYAL ENGINEERS
REX CHUBB	WOUNDED IN ACTION
LESLIE COATES	
BERT DRAYTON	R.A. MISSING, PRESUMED KILLED 1942
WYNDHAM DRAYTON	R.A.F.
ARTHUR DRUCE	R.A.S.C.
BERT DRUCE	SOM. L.I.
STANLEY DRUCE	SOM. L.I.
WYNDHAM DRUCE	R.A.
DENNIS GAYLARD	SOM. L.I.
PHILIP GAYLARD	R.N.
MAURICE GAYLARD	
FRED HOCKEY	R.A.F.
WILLIAM HOCKEY	
WILLIAM MASTERS	SOM. L.I.
RONALD MASTERS	GLOUCESTER REG.
COLIN OSBORNE	R.A.
DOUGLAS PILTON	R.N.
EDWARD RICHARDS	R.A.S.C.
ERNEST SHARP	
FRED SHARP	
WALTER SHARP	R.M.
JOHN SHARP	
ROY TROTT	SOM. L.I.
EDGAR TUCKER	P.O.W.
CYRIL WILTON	R.A.S.C.
REGINALD WILTON	SOM. L.I. KILLED IN ACTION AUG. 1944

Montacute Home Guard

The Montacute unit was formed as part of the Home Guard army; young men joined prior to being called up to the regular forces. Senior members of the community also joined the Home Guard. Some of the senior men had seen previous military service and could share with the younger members their experience of tactics in deployment and discipline, in the event of invasion.

The unit was brought up to strength and trained in the modern tactics of warfare, carrying out manoeuvres and exercises around Montacute, and testing each other's capabilities against other villages.

The exercises were carried out in the most realistic way possible. For instance, Bill Fall remembers being in the Home Guard and a battle scene of street fighting being staged in Bishopston in Montacute one Sunday morning. Men took cover in doorways. Then the officer in charge threw a thunderflash to signal the soldiers to open fire to start the battle. Bill's mother, then living in Bishopston, opened the bedroom window wondering what was happening and was alarmed to see bodies of men lying in the road. She thought they were dead, and was relieved to see them all get up after the exercises!

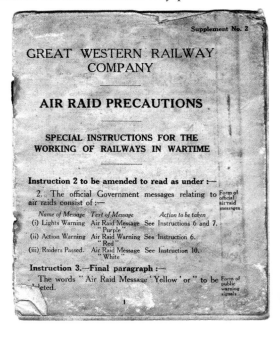

Another exercise was carried out at Bagnel, near Norton sub Hamdon. Bill was in the squad, operating the Lewis machine gun. He remembers walking up Hollow Lane carrying the Lewis gun magazines (which fitted on top of the gun) loaded with bullets. He said that by the time they marched up Hollow Lane and down through Witcombe Valley, his arms felt as if they were dropping off.

Humphrey Hamlin remembers the Home Guard practising grenade throwing in Montacute Recreation Field. He said the soldiers would sit in a little hut priming the grenades in case of sudden enemy action. He also remembers them practising defence tactics around Montacute Tower.

Hidden in the banks at the top of Hollow Lane, there were barrels of inflammable material. These could be ignited and ejected into the road against oncoming enemy vehicles.

Also in Hollow Lane, the author remembers seeing, as a young boy playing on the high banks, two dug out pits, square in shape, one each side of the lane. These, he believes, would have been used for defence purposes. Each could have contained a machine gun emplacement. Because of their high position, they would have had a commanding field of fire all over the village and surrounding countryside.

At the top of Hollow Lane and going past Batemore Barn on the right hand side, there is a field called "Dog Trap", partially shielded by a high hamstone cliff. This was used by the Home Guard as a firing range. The cliff face was a backdrop and support for targets.

Reginald (Dick) Hann lived at Townsend, Montacute, and was a member of the Home Guard. His daughter, Shirley Hann, remembers her father being called out to look for German airmen who had parachuted from their aircraft after being hit by anti-aircraft fire. He assisted in the capture of a German airman. Mr Hann also helped the Montacute Home Guard by tracing ordnance survey maps of the local area for use by members of the Home Guard because not enough original maps were available.

Reginald was a stonemason and worked for Appleby & Childs Monumental Masons in Yeovil. Here he helped the war effort by using his skills in grinding and polishing quartz plates. This was top secret work, the items produced being used in the detection of enemy submarines. When the plates were ready for use, they were transported by Appleby Childs' lorry, complete with armed guard, to Portland Naval Base. The idea was that a civilian lorry would help avoid the suspicion of spies and enemy agents.

Group of Memorial Masons taken at work, Appleby & Childs, Yeovil.

John Guppy, now living at Barwick, was an apprentice at Appleby & Childs, and has related to me the information about the A.S.D.I.C. (*Allied Submarine Detection Investigation Committee*) construction. He also knew Reginald (Dick) Hann. He recalls watching Dick sitting on his box, working stone, which was his normal trade. The work continued throughout the war. Appleby & Childs ceased trading at their premises in Middle Street Yeovil, in 1957.

Members of the Home Guard – some of the names given to the author

Mr Ewens	Bill Fall
Reg Hawkins	Frank Bartlett (Sgt)
Wyndham Drayton	Reginald Hann

Left: *Defence Medal as awarded to personnel of the Home Guard.*

Right: *Sgt Frank Bartlett, Home Guard with son Raymond.*

In the years when our Country

was in mortal danger

Sgt A.F. BARTLETT

who served   22 June 1940 – 31 December 1944

gave generously of his time and

powers to make himself ready

for her defence by force of arms

and with his life if need be.

George R.I.

THE HOME GUARD

Sgt Frank Bartlett certificate.

Sgt Frank Bartlett citation.

The Village Remembers

Memories of the Home Front and of those who served

Raymond Bartlett

Raymond Bartlett recalls that while attending Montacute School, all the pupils put their names on slips of paper and placed them in a hat and the winner attended a party held by the Americans at Houndstone Camp. Raymond was the lucky one and he remembers going to the party in the back of an American Army lorry.

Clarence Remembers

I can just remember, as a small boy living at Stoke sub Hamdon, having my first encounter with the American Forces.

I was sitting on the garden wall outside the house with another boy from the opposite side of the road, watching a convoy of American lorries and tracked vehicles going by.

The soldiers were generous – throwing sweets and chocolate to the children from the vehicles. Seizing the opportunity, I got off the wall and dashed to gather them up. Returning to my seat, I started to enjoy my rewards while continuing to watch the convoy going by. Suddenly a wasp came along and stung me on the arm and I ran into the house, crying.

Eventually our family moved to Montacute and we lived at Abbey Cottages, with my grandfather, who worked as a shepherd for Mr Hugh Cannon at Abbey Farm.

I started at Montacute School. Clutching my dinner money in one hand and an apple in the other, I entered the school. Your dinner money was placed inside a matchbox with your name suitably inscribed upon it and put upon a tray ready for collection by the lady who did the accounts and who also used to sell National Savings stamps on Fridays. The children saved the stamps till they eventually qualified for a savings certificate to the value of fifteen shillings or one pound.

We had regular morning services with my favourite hymns such as, "There is a Green Hill Far Away", and "Praise my Soul the King of Heaven". On some occasions the children were allowed to choose the hymns.

Register followed, when you went to your allotted classes. Afterwards, everyone had to put their hands up and be counted for the allocation of the daily bottle of milk which you drank with the aid of a straw.

Some excitement was had at this stage to see who could blow the most bubbles in the bottle, or to place a drop of milk upon the hot coke stove and see it dance across the hot-plate and give off an appalling odour for which we were reprimanded.

Our lessons comprised of the "three R's". Reading, writing and arithmetic, plus the Scriptures and Nature Study, the latter being my favourite lesson, especially the nature study walks we were taken on.

The desks at which we sat to learn our lessons were the old fashioned type with hinged seats and tops and a rail to rest your back against. The inkwells situated at the top end of the desk were kept filled by the child who was nominated as the ink monitor, who had at his or her disposal a large brown bottle as a constant reservoir of ink.

The school plays were always a great joy to perform which I enjoyed immensely every term. The partitions that divided the larger two classrooms were opened up to reveal the audience and players to each other. The audience was made up mostly of parents, who came along to see their children perform. The "actors" used to peer through the chinks of the doors before the play started to see if their particular parents were present. Their presence or absence either added to morale or caused despondency at that particular moment.

To reach the boys' playground, the children had to walk up a walled, protected path. How many noticed the engraved stone on the left hand side set in the wall? The carving depicts the sign of the fish. It presumably came from the old Abbey which was destroyed during the Reformation.

The railings at the front of the school, which surround the small garden, came from the old Ilchester jail. Imagine what memories and stories they could tell of the inmates which they secured, from murderers to sheep stealers! Outside the kitchen door, the deep grooves etched in the brickwork were left by the children of earlier years where they sharpened their slate scribers to enable them to write upon the slates.

To think what great changes have taken place in education – from its infancy to the present day, especially in our village school! For instance, progressing from scribing on slates to writing with pen and ink. The technical age has very much influenced the trend of teaching with the assistance of radio and television, and now that we are in the computer age – what will the future bring? Whatever the outcome, the village school will still have a major role to play.

My teacher, Miss Celia Bryant, told us various things about the war. One particular discussion was about when the Americans' tanks came through the village and damaged the pavement kerbstones, especially along Bishopston. These marks can still be seen today and are more prevalent in the blue lias stone kerbs, opposite Wash Lane.

The Author pointing at kerbstone damage caused by the American tanks, still visible today.

I also have memories of their military ambulances parked in the West Drive, nose to tail the whole length of the drive. The American embassy advised me that these ambulances would have belonged to the 159th General Hospital which was based in Yeovil.

The other Americans based in Montacute were most likely to have been the 97th Quartermaster Battalion, formed on 25 June 1942 at Camp Swift, Texas, U.S.A. It was reorganised and redesignated in 1943 as Headquarters Detachment, 97th Quartermaster Battalion.

I can remember the Nissen Huts at the entrance to the south side, adjacent to the yew tree hedge and the nursery garden. Montacute House was requisitioned to hold the art treasures from the Victoria and Albert Museum for safe keeping during the war.

However, when the German air force started to bomb the towns of Southern England, it was decided that Montacute House was too vulnerable. In 1942 the contents were moved to underground caverns below Corsham in Wiltshire (which were also drier and more moth free than Montacute).

During the war a committee was formed under Sir Geoffrey Hippisley-Cox to arrange for the use of the house after the war. Lord Aberconway was to advise on the care of the garden and H. Clifford-Smith on the collections. Before the war the house had been shown virtually unfurnished, but it was felt that this was detrimental to the property maintaining itself financially, besides constituting a waste of space which was potentially valuable for cultural and educational purposes.

As a result of a letter published in *The Times* on 11 April 1945, generous benefactors offered fine pieces from their collections. When the house was reopened on 20 July 1946, seven principal rooms were furnished. Among the first acquisitions was the remarkable Gamlen bed of 1612, presented by J. C. B. Gamlen.

I have in my possession a pair of American soldier's leggings which I purchased at a local sale. The numbers printed inside related to the makers who were the Bray Co. and they were distributed through the Jeffersonville Quartermaster Depot, Jeffersonville, Indiana, U.S.A.

I am grateful to Janet Jenkins for granting access to the Abbey Farm Gatehouse roof. It was a flat roof to make it easily accessible for maintenance. It also allowed American servicemen to engrave their names in the

26

leadwork, so my photographer, Philip Hodges and I took some photographs
of the signatures to put on record. The names were:—

L KERR 1944

L BM VISONE 1944

HARRY HANIM JNR USA 1944 MICHIGAN

RYAN ELEY 1944

ALLEN CHRISTIAN, MEMPHIS, TENESSEE USA 9-7-1944

HARRY HAMILTON 6-4-1944

(The coins used to give an idea of size are 1p.)

Harry S. Hamilton

One of the names on the Abbey Gatehouse roof is that of Harry S. Hamilton. He was born in Battle Creek, Michigan, U.S.A. in 1910, and was a lifelong resident of Battle Creek.

When America entered the war, Harry enlisted (1 May 1943) and served in the Medical Department in Europe, reaching the rank of Sergeant.

When the war ended, Harry returned to Battle Creek and was employed by the General Foods Corporation as a painter, retiring in 1973 after thirty-seven years' service.

Harry died in 1981 in Provincial House where he had been a patient for three years. Harry's wife died in 1977.

This inscription is from Pte John Osgood US Army and is located on the right side of the old kitchen doorway of Montacute House.

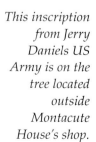

This inscription from Jerry Daniels US Army is on the tree located outside Montacute House's shop.

There are also many inscriptions from this period on and inside Montacute Tower on St Michael's Hill.

Clarence pointing at one of the inscriptions on Montacute Tower.

Names Given to the Author, in the Visitors' Books, the King's Arms

Names from the Visitors' Books of the King's Arms Hotel, Montacute

2.1.44	Vincent G. Tuttle, NYC, USA
3.1.44	George H. Macary, Roselle, NJ, USA
2.3.44	Lt Albert B. Vallelanga, US Army
	ORA G. Tucker, US Army
2.4.44	Lt Leroy Hearlman, US Army CAC AWS
4.4.44	Lt Aris R. Plantsman, USA
	Patterson, Glassbord NJ, US Army

Walter Stanley Barnett
Signalman Royal Signals

Walter Stanley Barnett, best known as "Bill", was born 11 January 1924 in Northampton. He attended school there and later worked as a trainee electrician wireman for the Northampton Electric Light Company.

In 1943, aged nineteen, Bill volunteered for the forces because all his other friends were joining and he felt he ought to enlist. His basic training was carried out at Glasgow Highland Light Infantry, and lasted six weeks. Afterwards he was posted to Catterick to be trained as a wireless operator and this training took twenty-one weeks.

45 Squad, No. 2 Coy., 1 O.T.Bn., R. Signals — Jan. 1944

Back Row—Signalmen Burke,   Harbridge,   Lee,   Simpson,   Tarr,   French,
Centre Row—Signalmen Davie,   Lansley,   Chambers,   Lister,   Munday,   Buckingham,   Onyett,   Barnett.
Front Row—Signalmen Palmer,   Bond,   Bayley,   L/Cpl Laidlaw,   Cpl Miller (Instructor)   Signalmen Blackmore,   Bell,   Butley.

In May 1944, Bill was posted to Leeds Castle in Kent, being billeted in Nissen huts. He later joined the 53rd Welsh Division (Territorials).

In June 1944, the Division was detailed to Tilbury Dock to take part in the "D Day" landings at Normandy, known as "Operation Overlord". Bill, together with his radio lorry, landed from a landing craft on "D Day +4" at Arromanches and drove inland, but resistance held the Division up at Caen. Later Bill drove his radio truck further inland, pushing on against enemy forces.

Bill remarked that his 15 cwt truck was known as a gin palace because on occasions the officers used it as a cocktail bar and meeting place.

The Division continued into Belgium and on to Brussels. It was here that Bill's unit was requested to help the Americans at the "Battle of the Bulge" in the Ardennes. The weather was bitterly cold. Bill's radio lorry, together with another lorry, was positioned in the forest and the driver of the second vehicle decided to light a fire for a brew up. This was not a wise move as smoke curled up through the trees, giving the position away. The Germans spotted the smoke and zeroed in on it; a German Tiger tank opened fire with its 88 mm gun and placed a shell between the two lorries. Bill was hit in the leg by the shell blast. He said that if it had been shrapnel, he would have lost his leg.

Bill was taken to a military hospital for treatment. It happened to be his twenty-first birthday when he was operated on. He was sent to a transit camp to recover and eventually caught up with his unit in Holland. This was the same year as "Operation Market Garden" took place – the airborne invasion of Holland at Arnhem.

[Incidentally, my uncle was a glider pilot at Arnhem and survived – Author.]

When the war ended, Bill and his unit had reached Hamburg in Germany.

He was posted back to England and home. After leave he was attached to Unit 2 Air Support Signal Unit on 4 September 1946. He was posted to Palestine, and attached to RAF Air Support with Typhoon aircraft. In the event of emergency, Bill could call up the aircraft for an air strike on a particular target.

Bill spent some time in Jerusalem, setting up a radio link with Haifa. He had a second lucky escape while there. One day when off duty he was on a lorry travelling along the road when he heard an explosion, and stopping to look, discovered that a terrorist had blown up the hotel Bill had just left.

Bill was released from the Army at Pocklington in 1947 with a first class reference from his commanding officer.

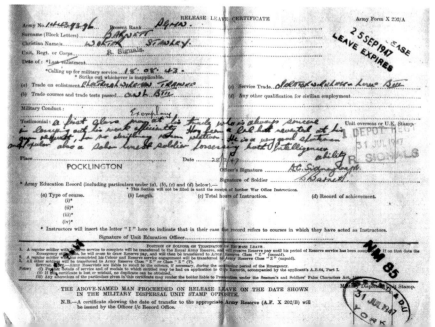

Leslie Brimble
Royal Artillery
Army No 1599309

Leslie (Les) Brimble was born in Montacute in 1916. On leaving Montacute School, Les trained as a leather dresser and worked for Whitbys and Pittards in Yeovil.

At the outbreak of war Les joined the Royal Artillery and enlisted at Watchet, Somerset on 15 July 1940. He trained as a gunner with the Royal Artillery, eventually being posted to the Middle East where he served from 16 December, 1940 to 28 May, 1941. Les was captured on 29 May, 1941 and was a prisoner of war in Stalag VIIIH in Germany until released on 29 May, 1945.

The photograph opposite shows Les standing on the right with his fellow prisoners of war. On the back of the photograph (opposite below) is the official German prison camp identification stamp.

When Les was first captured and transported to Germany as a prisoner, he recalls the lack of food and drink. He said, "some of the prisoners had to drink their own urine". After the war, at meal times he would often tell his family not to waste food, saying that the scraps on their plates would have been appreciated by his fellow prisoners of war.

Les's father was the local policeman in Montacute during the war and Les told Carol, his daughter, how his father would keep a wary eye on everyone during the war, especially when items were scarce.

Mr Brimble and his wife had an American nurse staying with them during the war, whose name was Malt. She was stationed at the American 159th General Hospital at Lufton Camp, Yeovil and some of the first casualties from the Normandy landings were evacuated there. Malt was involved in their recovery. After the war Malt returned to America but kept in touch with Mr and Mrs Brimble. She sent some American money to Mrs Brimble which Chris, Mrs Brimble's grandson, has to this day.

Les was discharged from the Army on the 9 February, 1946, with a total service of five years and 210 days. He was awarded the 1939-1943 Star.

Captain Stanley Norman Burfield MBE
4th Battalion Somerset Light Infantry

Norman Burfield was born in Montacute to parents John and Edna. He was one of five children and lived at 40 Townsend, in 1919.

Norman grew up in the village and attended Montacute School. On passing a scholarship, Norman went to Yeovil Grammar School.

Norman hated school. He was particularly good at sport, especially cricket, but not interested in lessons. He was selected to play in the 1st cricket XI scoring a large number of runs for the team. During one particular match he amassed a great score. After Norman had walked back to the pavilion the sports master said, "well done Burfield, but don't hit the ball in the air – keep it on the ground". Norman's remark was not polite and he was reported to the Headmaster. On being disciplined by the Headmaster, Norman apparently said, "I am walking out of here and not coming back to school" – which he did, so he never received his school colours for playing in the 1st team.

Eventually the family moved to St Michael's View opposite the recreation field. Norman sought work and found employment at Hunt's Glove Factory, East Street, Martock and started training as a glove cutter.

Norman joined the Territorial Army in 1939 and served in the ranks as a private, eventually achieving the rank of Sergeant.

It was in the Territorials in 1939 that Norman came to know Charles Marshalsea, also from Montacute, who later became Norman's vehicle driver. Charles joined the Somerset Light Infantry as a Territorial and was called up in 1939. He was one of the first to go to war from Montacute and was then living at 35 Yeovil Road. During his time in the Army, Charles served in Italy. He was released from the Army in 1945 but still remained friends with Norman.

Charlie Marshalsea
Somerset Light Infantry TA

Charles remained in Montacute (eventually living in Lower Hyde Road) initially working for Mr Brown the coalman who lived in Montacute Borough and used the coal yard at Montacute Station. After leaving Mr Brown's employment, Charles spent the rest of his working life at Mr Rex Drayton's Myrtle Farm at Back Lane, Montacute. Charles died in 1979 at the age of seventy-four.

In 1941 Norman married Molly at Ilminster, Somerset and they were an ideally suited couple. In 1942, Norman was selected for officer training at Sandhurst. He later became an Adjutant of 4th Somerset Light Infantry.

Norman was posted to Dover

Charlie at work in the 1950s.

Norman and Molly Burfield.

to assist in planning and intelligence operations for "D Day". He landed at Arromanches. After the breakout of the beach head the regiment moved inland and engaged with the enemy. During the action Norman was wounded and was evacuated to a military hospital in London. While recovering from his wounds in hospital he was placed in a padded cell, to aid the recovery of his nerves and reduce the effects of shock, as the nurses' grey uniforms had brought back feelings of fear and dread as Norman had associated them with the German uniforms of field grey from the battlefield.

When the war finished in 1945 he became a teacher at Stoke Secondary Modern School, now known as Stanchester Academy. After a while Norman left teaching and went back to the gloving trade. Norman started his own business in the gloving trade in 1947 under the name of Burfield Glove and Martock Glove Company.

Later Norman became President of Yeovil Town Football Club and also President of Montacute Cricket Club. He was also awarded the MBE.

Kenneth Frederick Bussell
2113242 Royal Engineers

Ken volunteered for the Royal Air Force but was not accepted. Undeterred, Ken volunteered for the Army and was accepted and joined the Royal Engineers. He enlisted at Bordon on 27 June, 1940. Ken trained as a driver.

He recalls his first day of hard work, digging tank traps with a pick and shovel in case of invasion. His first day out on 6 July 1940, was to Farnham, a distance of 6 to 7 miles, travelling by Aldershot & District Traction Company's Dennis diesel bus, painted dark and light green.

2

(1) SOLDIER'S NAME and DESCRIPTION on ATTESTATION.

Army Number _____ *2113242* _____

Surname (in capitals) _____ *BUSSELL.* _____

Christian Names (in full) *KENNETH FREDERICK*

Date of Birth _____ *4 . 5 . 20* .

Trade on Enlistment *LEATHER WORKER (GEN)*

Religious Denomination _____ *C of E.*

Approved Society _____ *Nat. Deposit*

Membership No. _____ *43.19.495436*

Enlisted at *BORDON* _____ On *27. 6 . 40*

For the :—

　　* Regular Army. 　　　* Supplementary Reserve.
　　* Territorial Army. 　* Army Reserve Section D.
　　　　* Strike out those inapplicable.

For _____ years with the Colours and _____ years in the Reserve.

　　Signature of Soldier _____

Date _____

3

DESCRIPTION ON ENLISTMENT.

Height _____ *5* _____ ft. *10½* ins. Weight *110* _____ lbs.

Maximum Chest *30½* ins. Complexion *FRESH*

Eyes _____ *D. BROWN* _____ Hair _____ *DARK*

Distinctive Marks and Minor Defects _____

A & S GRO. 31c   C.D. Comidien Maj

CONDITION ON TRANSFER TO RESERVE.

Found fit for _____ *"B. L. A. I"*

Defects or History of past illness which should be enquired into if called up for Service _____

Date _____ 19 _____

Initials of M.O. i/c. _____

In July, while he was trench digging, the first German aircraft passed overhead. They were being chased by Spitfires travelling at high speed. On Sunday 21 July, Ken visited Petersfield. He had tea at the Drill Hall canteen and met Jimmy Shoemark, also from Montacute, who had just returned from leave.

On 1 August, having finished his training, Ken moved to Longmoor Camp. On 13 August, Ken experienced German air raids by dive bombers. About 50 bombs were dropped on or near the railway line. "Most of us," he said, "thought they were British planes, but they were soon identified as enemy aircraft." The same day, there was a very bad air raid on the camp, three or four huts were hit and burnt to the ground. It was massed attacks everywhere that day. He added "on 24 August I went to Petersfield with my new chum, Doug Yeadon, and we wrote our letters home under a gorse bush owing to a very heavy air raid on Portsmouth." On Friday 30 August, Ken was detailed as an observer on the water tower which he did for forty-eight hours. He must have seen great numbers of aircraft in the air.

On 5 September 1940, Ken moved to Paignton, Devon, a long journey by train which took all day, due to the wartime conditions. "Walking out the first time in Paignton, we had to carry rifles and ten rounds of ammunition with us owing to an invasion scare," he recalls.

Ken remembers driving his first Army vehicle around Paignton accompanied by his instructor, Lance Corporal French.

On 23 October 1940, everyone was dressed in full pack by 9.30 a.m. and moved to Fowey, Cornwall. "The weather was not good when we arrived at Fowey and travelled the extra 4 miles to our billet, St Catherine's Hotel, right on top of the cliffs. The sea provided a magnificent spectacle. We were assigned to various duties including cleaning vehicles and cookhouse tasks."

Friday 1 November, Ken notes, "informed of another transfer to the Plymouth detachment and had to start packing again. I did not like that very much owing to frequent air raids. We had a half hour bus journey to Par Station – arrived at Plymouth 5.45 p.m."

Ken's next posting was to London, billeted in Upper Grosvenor Street, practically opposite Grosvenor House – rather posh, owing to it being in Mayfair. Ken was involved with rescue work on bombed buildings which was very unpleasant, especially finding bodies.

He continues " On 27 November I had my first leave from joining the

Royal Engineers, leaving Waterloo Station at 5 p.m. and arriving home at 10.30 p.m. My parents were overjoyed to see me. I enjoyed my leave at home, went for some good walks with my brother and visited the glove factory where I used to work as a leather sorter and clerk. I also had a talk with Mr Southcombe, the factory owner. He gave me 10/- before saying farewell. Also received 100 cigarettes from the employees.

I returned to London and continued with demolition work. We were issued with new overalls and paraded in Grosvenor Square with inspection, and then marched to work headed by a fife and drum band."

It was also in London that Ken was able to pursue his love of music and to seize every opportunity to visit shows, theatres and cinemas.

On Sunday 29 December, Ken was in London's first big fire blitz, a large blaze lighting up miles of streets. It happened all around St Paul's Cathedral, and especially in some big warehouses nearby.

Sunday 19 January 1941 – "We had a loot inspection. No-one was caught for thieving. I left Waterloo Station at 4 p.m. for forty-eight hours home leave".

On Saturday 8 March 1941, Ken went to the Regal cinema, in Edmonton. "While enjoying the film, guns and bombs were making a devil of a noise. I managed to get home safely although some of the aircraft swooped very low which made us run a bit fast."

Saturday 10 May 1941 Ken adds "I experienced one of the worst raids over London, starting at 11 p.m. and finishing at 5.50 a.m. on the Sunday morning. 300 to 400 planes were estimated to have been involved, 33 of them being brought down. I had to stay up all night fire watching while screaming bombs were dropping around us. One dropped near at hand breaking plenty of windows in the streets. The raid was concentrated on the West End where we were billeted."

On 3 June 1941 Ken continues, "I had seven days' leave – left London and arrived at Yeovil at 12 p.m. I walked the whole distance from Yeovil to Montacute. A chap caught me up at Houndstone Bridge and helped me with my kit. My leave ended and I was seen off at the station at Yeovil by my mother and Ron."

Tuesday 24 June 1941 – "I was told to pack and get ready to move to Scotland on detachment. I was glad, owing to it being a change of scenery. We packed everything, left Kings Cross, London, and arrived in Edinburgh. There we caught a train to Shandon, Dunbartonshire. After settling in, I had a day off and paid a visit to Helensburgh, travelling on an old bus built in

1928. Bus service rather out of date for times."

On 29 June 1941 – "Started work on the big job at Faslane Quay, erecting big cranes for the purpose of unloading ships. Rations were brought to the job – sandwiches, Swiss roll and an orange."

Monday 14 July 1941 Ken adds, "I drove Captain Catterall and Major Purues to a Military Hospital which was formerly Dryner Castle. This is where Rudolph Hess was convalescing after landing by aeroplane in this country. He was at that time the third leading light in the Nazi party. Also there, were prisoners from the German pocket battleship, *Bismarck*, being cared for by Red Cross Nurses. It was when we were working on the lock I witnessed the crash of a Flying Boat which was being tested near us."

Ken had more leave on 18 November 1941. "I left Shandon at 7.58 a.m. for the long journey to Somerset. After numerous changes, eventually arrived at Taunton at 11.30 p.m. After about six cups of tea, I slept in the waiting room and on Wednesday morning, 19th November, I was awakened by a porter at Taunton Station to catch the train for Montacute at 7.10 a.m. eventually arriving at Montacute at 8.10 a.m."

29 November 1941 – "I started from Montacute Station at 7.50 a.m., travelling by GWR from Taunton back to Scotland, getting back to the camp at midnight thoroughly tired and exhausted ."

25 December 1941 – Christmas Day – "Had a smashing time. After the church service at Helensburgh, visited the Imperial Hotel along the front, drinking whisky and beer. I was rather merry. We had a lovely Xmas dinner with plenty of beer and after the meal enjoyed a nice cigar."

As the old year was passing out on 31 December 1941, all the ships that were in convoy blew their sirens till after midnight to welcome the new year.

Ken was posted overseas to North Africa in 1942 and while driving up through the desert on the coastal road in convoy, he witnessed a ship blowing up out at sea.

He describes it as a huge explosion, the ship seemed to be lifted up in the air and when the water settled there was absolutely nothing – just floating pieces of debris.

After the Desert Campaign, Ken returned to the UK and took part in the landings in Normandy.

He landed on 7 June and drove his lorry off the ship, onto the beach where he got bogged down in the sand and had to be winched up the beach

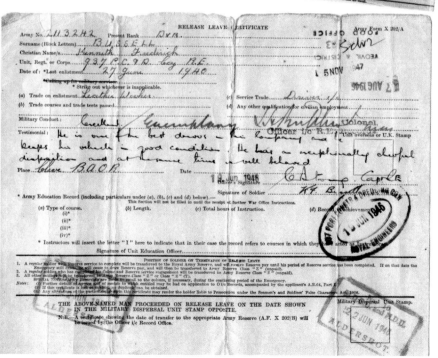

to solid ground before moving inland.

He remembers digging a slit trench to sleep in at night beside the lorry by the side of the road, and further progress into France, receiving some incoming fire. He remembers crossing the Pegasus Bridge.

The facilities were sparse and he always told the family about having a bath with the aid of a biscuit tin containing water.

Ken named his lorry "Yeovil", and his wife said, "he put a card on his windscreen saying YEOVIL" so that any soldiers on route who were from Somerset seeing this would come and make themselves known.

Ken was awarded the North African Campaign Medal – the Africa Star, with the first Army Clasp, 1942-43, and was discharged from the Army on 19 June 1946.

Douglas Carswell

I visited Doug Carswell, now living at Yetminster in Dorset, and he spoke to me about living at the Vicarage in Montacute as a young lad during the war. The vicar at the time was the Reverend Beechey. The author remembers going to Sunday School after the war at St Catherine's church, Montacute, and being given the Best Attendance Prize by Reverend Beechey.

Doug remembers attending Montacute School and vividly recalls having to lie down on a small coconut mat after lunch, to rest. He also says that the boys' toilets were up on the top playground and the pupils had to walk along the enclosed hamstone passage way in all winds and weathers.

In the winter months, Doug tells of sledging down St Michael's Hill, going so fast that he shot straight over the surrounding wall and landed in the next field.

Doug also describes walking around the neighbouring fields with the other boys, during the war, gathering shiny metal foil strips dropped by the German aircraft. The Germans used these as jamming devices to try to prevent the detection of their raids by British radar installations.

A pleasant time was had by Doug while playing in Montacute recreation field. His favourite activity was spinning round on the roundabout with the other children. While playing in the field one day, a convoy of American lorries passed through the village in the direction of Stoke sub Hamdon and the soldiers threw out sweets to the children. Doug also recalls American soldiers sitting on the seats in the Recreation Field with their girlfriends, and the village boys teasing them.

The soldiers would have come from Montacute Park where they lived in Nissen huts. These soldiers also went on route marches and marched through the village and all around Ham Hill. Doug remembers the sergeant who led them being called Sergeant Asher.

Doug also remembers paddling in the sheep wash in Lower Town, and watching the trains. He spoke of the time when the German aircraft dropped bombs near the station and near Stoke School.

Doug left Montacute towards the end of the war and went to live in Bower Hinton. He still visits Montacute with his grandchildren and tells them what the village was like when he was young.

Flight Engineer Sergeant J. H. Chant
Royal Air Force

Jack joined the Royal Air Force in 1940. After basic training he was posted to Brasted in Kent where he was engaged in recovering crashed aircraft. Jack was part of a team, sometimes staying at RAF bases in Kent, sometimes

being billeted in people's houses in the neighbourhood. Whenever the call came in about a downed aircraft, they would set out with a van for transporting personnel and a "Queen Mary" aircraft recovery lorry and trailer. The team dismantled the aircraft and any good components were used as replacement parts for other aircraft.

Jack describes the crew as a good lot of blokes, always helping one another. He remembers one particular mate called Larry Wright who owned a Singer car. Eight of them would pile into the

No: 425 (RCAF) Sqdn   66567 1
Tholthorpe

Certificates of Qualification.
(to be filled in as appropriate)   Sgt

Instructions.

1. This log book is an official document and the property of H.M. Government.

2. This log book is to be maintained by all members of air crew other than pilot. An accurate record of all flights under-taken on service aircraft is to be inserted.

3. Results of ab initio courses will be recorded on either pages 2, 3, 4 or 5, for which purpose a rubber stamp is available.

4. Proficiency assessments will be recorded on the appropriate page at the back of the book on posting or on attachment to another unit for flying duties.

5. Bombing and Air Gunnery records will be entered in detail in the appropriate pages at the end of the book immediately after each practice.

6. Monthly totals will be entered on a single line in red ink and initialled by the Commanding Officer or his deputy.

1. This is to certify that **N° 1244596. CHANT. J.A.** has qualified as **F/ENG.** with effect from **4·12·43.** Sgd. Date ____ Unit **ST. ATHAN.**

2. This is to certify that ____ has qualified as ____ with effect from ____ Sgd. ____ Date ____ Unit ____

3. This is to certify that ____ has qualified as ____ with effect from ____ Sgd. ____ Date ____ Unit ____

4. This is to certify that ____ has qualified as ____ with effect from ____ Sgd. ____ Date ____ Unit ____

Jack Chant's qualification certificate.

car and go out to the local pub.

In 1943, Jack applied for training as aircrew and was accepted and trained at RAF St Athans. He qualified as a Flight Engineer with the rank of Sergeant with effect from 4 December 1943. Jack was posted to 1664 CU Dishforth, Yorkshire, training on Halifax bombers.

Eventually Jack joined 425 Squadron in April 1944, flying in Halifax bombers from Tholthorpe. Jack's crew flew six operational bombing raids before being shot down on an operation over Haines St Pierre in Belgium.

After rendezvousing over the North Sea with other squadrons, some 100 aircraft headed for the railway marshalling yards at Haines St Pierre, It was a clear moonlit night and the target was located and attacked without problems. The eight man crew of the Halifax, six French Canadians, an American pilot and Jack, headed for home.

Flying at some 16,000 feet, just to the south of Ghent, they were attacked

425. SQUADRON. APRIL. 1944.

Time carried forward :— 55:30 14:50.

Date	Hour	Aircraft Type and No.	Pilot	Duty	Remarks (including results of bombing, gunnery, exercises, etc.)		Flying Times	
							Day	Night
10:4:44	10:30.	K. HALIFAX	4/LT. BRYSON. F/SGT. WHITE.	ENGINEER.	G. & L.	D.C.O.	1:20.	
10:4:44	12:00.	K.	P/S. WHITE.	"	LOCAL FLYING.	D.C.O.	1:00.	
11:4:44	20:00	LW 232. J.	F/SGT. WHITE.	"	X COUNTRY.	D.C.O.		5:00.
12:4:44	18:00	LW 176. R.	F/SGT. WHITE.	"	X COUNTRY.	D.C.O.		3:10.
13:4:44	10:30	LW. 415. K.	F/LT. BRYSON.	"	BASE - LINTON.	D.C.O.	:30.	
22:4:44	10:15.	L.W. -G.	F/O. WHITE.	"	BOMBING. & LOCAL. FLYING.	D.N.C.O.		
23:4:44	14:10.	L.W. - G.	F/O. WHITE.	"	F/A. & BOMBING.	D.CO.	1:20.	
26:4:44	23:05	L.W. - S.	F/O. WHITE.	"	OPS. ESSEN.	D.C.O		5:05.
27:4:44	00:00	L.W. - S.	F/O. WHITE.	"	OPS. AULNOYE.	D.C.O		4:50.

TOTAL HOURS DAY: 4: 10.
TOTAL HOURS NIGHT 18: 5.
GRAND TOTAL: 22 : 15.

TOTAL TIME ...59:40 32:55

124596. SGT. CHANT. J.

1664 C.U. DISHFORTH, YORKS.

Time carried forward :—

Date	Hour	Aircraft Type and No.	Pilot	Duty	Remarks (including results of bombing, gunnery, exercises, etc.)		Flying Times	
							Day	Night
30.12.44	09:20	HALIFAX DH - H.	F/O. FINCH.	2nd. ENG.	DUAL. EX: 3 & 4.	D.C.O.	2: 10.	
6.1.44	10.45.	HALIFAX ZU-C.	F/SGT. WHITE.	2nd. ENG.	CROSS COUNTRY.	D.C.O.	4: 15.	
19.1.44	09:45	HALIFAX DH-W.	S/LDR. PETERSON. 2/LDR. PETERSON.	ENG.	FAMIL. G. & L.	D.C.O.	2:00.	
22.1.44	16:15.	HALIFAX DH-W.	F/SGT. ST. PIERRE. 2/LDR. PETERSON	ENG.	G. & L.	D.C.C.	2: 15.	
23.1.44	16:10.	HALIFAX DH-Z.	F/SGT. ST. PIERRE. F/O. GALLWN.	ENG.	G. & L.	D.C.C.	2:00.	
24.1.44	04:45	HALIFAX DH - W.	F/SGT. ST. PIERRE. 2/LDR. PETERSON	ENG.	G. & L.	D.N.C.O.	:15.	
27.1.44.	04:20.	HALIFAX DH-Z.	F/SGT. ST. PIERRE. S/LDR. PETERSON.	ENG.	G. & L.	U.N.C.O.	1 :15.	
30.1.44.	14.10.	HALIFAX DH-V.	F/SGT. ST. PIERRE. LT. CLARR.	ENG.	G. & L.	D.C.O.	2:00	
31.1.44.	14.05.	HALIFAX DH-X.	F/SGT. ST. PIERRE. F/O. FINCH.	ENG.	CHECK - DUAL.	D.C.C.	2: 45.	
5.2.44.	14.40.	HALIFAX DH-X	F/SGT. NARUM. F/O.	ENG.	FAMIL. G & L.	D.C.O.	3:00.	
15.2.44	16:30.	HALIFAX DH-J.	F/SGT. 174 ADAM.	ENG.	EX: 6. 7. & 8.	D.C.O.	3:30.	
18.2.44	11.25	ZU-K.	F/SGT. JOHNSTON.	ENG.	SEA SEARCH. OPS.	D.C.O.	4:50	
11.3.44	14.50	HALIFAX DH-C. F/O. QUEEN.	M/SGT. WHITE.	ENG.	FAMIL. G & L.	D.C.O.	3:25.	
12.3.44	09.50	HALIFAX DH-C. F/O. QUEEN.	M/SGT. WHITE.	ENG.	EX: 2 & 5. DUAL & SOLO. SINK FLYING	D.C.O.	3:30.	
13.3.44	14.40.	HALIFAX DH-C. F/O. QUEEN.	M/SGT. WHITE.	ENG.	EX: 6. 7. & 8. 3 " LANDING	D.C.O.	3:20.	
15.3.44	14. 10.	HALIFAX DH-B. F/O. QUEEN.	M/SGT. WHITE.	ENG.		D.C.O.	1:00.	
18.3.44	14. 50.	DH-G. F/O. QUEEN.	M/SGT. WHITE.	ENG.	G & L. 3 MORE. LANDING DUE & SOLO.	D.C.O.		3 : 10.
14.3.44	09:55	ZU-K. HALIFAX	M/SGT. WHITE.	ENG.	SEA SEARCH. OPS.	D.C.O.	4:55.	
20.3.44	14:55.	DH-N HALIFAX	M/SGT. WHITE.	ENG.	BOMBING.	D.C.O.	2: 15.	
20.3.44	16.30	ZU-G. HALIFAX	M/SGT. WHITE.	ENG.	X COUNTRY.	D.C.O.		5 : 35.
21.3.44	14.15.	ZU-J.	M/SGT. WHITE.	ENG.	X COUNTRY.	D.C.O.		6 : 05.

TOTAL TIME ... 49:10 14 : 50.

by a German ME110. The port inner engine immediately caught fire and, despite the crew's efforts, the plane began to dive. One of the wings became engulfed in flame and the order came to bail out. Jack was the sixth and last to parachute away from the crippled Halifax. He was later to learn that the pilot and navigator died in the wreckage.

Common practice amongst the aircrews at the time was to wear two or three pairs of trousers, tucked into their flying boots, to keep out the cold at high altitude. Jack, however, found that his place in the plane was quite warm so he was wearing just the one pair. As he glided to earth his boots flew off and disappeared into the darkness.

Standing in a Belgian field wearing only his white socks and a pair of chamois leather gloves (and his flying suit!) he began to haul in the billowing silk 'chute with the intention of burying it nearby. As Jack set about his task, several dogs began to bark nearby. Fearing imminent capture at the hands of the Germans, he left the 'chute and made a run for it. He kept on the move throughout the night until, around dawn, he holed up in a barn. Exhausted, he curled up in a pony trap and was soon asleep…

Towards the end of that day, an old man appeared around the side of the barn but when Jack beckoned to him he turned tail and hurried away. Another night, moving quietly through the dark countryside, brought Jack to another barn, where this time he was able to make himself comfortable in the hay loft. Feeling thirsty in the morning, he ventured down into the cow stalls looking for some water. He had seen the farmer working around the farm yard but had not expected to come face to face with his four year old daughter. Her cries alerted the whole family.

Monsieur Vande Ghinste-Vanhuesebrouck farmed in the village of Rolleghem with his wife, daughter and eighteen year old son, Germaine. Friendly though they were, the farmer explained that the Germans had visited the farm the day before searching for the allied airmen. The family had been warned that should they attempt to aid an escape they would be shot. It was agreed that, after a hearty meal and the swapping of names and addresses, the local German command would be telephoned.

Shortly after, Jack was led into custody by a German officer and three guards. After periods of interrogation locally and at headquarters in Brussels, he was eventually taken to the notorious Sagan Stalag Luft III P.O.W. camp on the German/Polish border. While Jack was at the prison camp, the prisoners kept up morale by annoying the guards, repeatedly asking to go to the ablutions and complaining about the lack of washing facilities. The prisoners helped one another to survive.

When the Russian army approached Sagan, around 10,000 P.O.W.s, including Jack, were immediately marched off through the forests of Poland, Czechoslovakia and into Germany on "the Long March" a journey that took weeks, in the harshest winter conditions, up to -25C temperatures, with little food or shelter. Many died during the march but Jack was a fighter and determined to survive.

In such severe conditions, with very little to eat, rampant disease, including pneumonia, and many deaths, it was the bond with his fellow men that he remembered most fondly. They seized any opportunity to lighten the mood.

In later years he loved to relive stories like the day two of his mates decided to heat some water in a container at the roadside to take a much needed bath, only to be strafed by friendly fire from the air, which sent them into the brambles with not a stitch on.

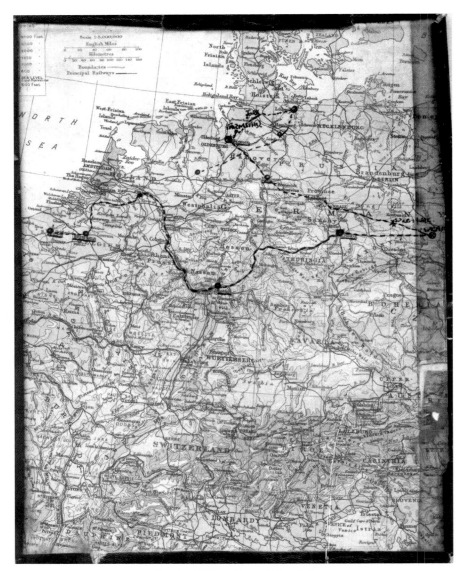

Route of "The Long March".

The camp they were moved to was liberated twelve months later on 4th May 1945. RAF Bomber Command implemented "Operation Exodus" and the first prisoners of war were repatriated by air. Bomber Command flew 2900 sorties over the next twenty three days, carrying 72,500 prisoners of war.

Date	Hour	Aircraft Type and No.	Pilot	Duty	Remarks (including results of bombing, gunnery, exercises, etc.)	Flying Times Day	Night
					Time carried forward :—	61:40	40:00
		LANC.					
9.5.45.	12.55.	S.		PASSENGER.	Return from Germany. (Riga.)	3.05.	
					TOTAL HOURS DAY: 64:45.		
					TOTAL HOURS NIGHT: 40:00.		
					GRAND TOTAL 104:45 HRS.		
11.7.53.		DAe.	PASSENGER	To Guernsey		1.00.	
18.7.53		RAPID	"	England.		1.00.	
3.7.93			"	Guernsey.		0.55	
7.7.93			"	England.		1.05	
					TOTAL TIME		

War ended and Jack was finally returned to the UK and de-mobbed. He travelled home to Yeovil and arrived whilst his mother was out walking his beloved dog, Shan, a mad red setter. His mother's joy at his return was only surpassed by Shan who, to Jack's great amusement, raced around the house, leaping the furniture in his excitement.

Jack met Elsie Asling at a dance and they were married in the summer of 1953 in Stoke sub Hamdon. They moved to Montacute in 1960 and brought up their two children, Jo and Tim.

Jack was proud of his family. Typical of the simple fun they enjoyed were the long summer evenings when Jack would often, after work, take his family to swim at Durdle Door, with fish and chips as a treat on the way home.

After one visit to stay with his son, Tim, and his wife Lynda, Jack mentioned how especially proud he was of his son as a new dad.

Both Jack and Elsie were tremendously proud in later years of their three grandsons, Ollie, Jacob and Toby. I know they all think very fondly of their grandfather and remember the happy, joking man they enjoyed visiting.

Jack was always delighted to see his nieces and nephews, to enjoy an ice cream on Ham Hill with Doreen, or have a long chat with Lesley to plan another adventure. Jack and Elsie loved Montacute and treasured their wonderful neighbours who were true friends to them, especially in the last few years.

Tim's in-laws, Pauline and John had friends living in Belgium. They invited Jack and Elsie to join them on a short holiday there one summer.

On 7 August Jack crossed the channel, by sea this time, and arrived in Belgium. On the second day it was agreed that the party should search for Jack's farmyard at Rolleghem. Out came the map, the village was located and off they went. A short time later they arrived in a quiet little village and parked outside the church while Jack went into a small delicatessen to seek directions. The shop owner was very helpful and pored through the local telephone directory for the Ghinste-Vanhuesbrouck family (not a name you could easily miss!), but to no avail. She then realised that Jack had mistaken her village of Rolleghem-Kappelle for Rolleghem.

Back to the car and away to an equally quiet little village. A young man approached the car and asked if he could help. When the surname was repeated, he recognised it immediately – relatives of his wife! He took the group to a converted barn and knocked on the door. A man answered, took one look at Jack and said, "John Harry Chant, Somerset." After that, tears of joy flowed as did several bottles of wine – German of course!

The man at the door was the farmer's son, Germaine, now aged seventy-one years. His father had unfortunately died some seven years before. Germaine took Jack and Elsie back to the old farmyard which had sheltered Jack that night and the memories of having to bale out and the loss of his fellow aircrew came flooding back.

55,000 aircrew in Bomber Command failed to return from missions during the Second World War.

Jack was one of the last of a generation who bravely fought to defend the liberty and freedom of this country. There are few left to recount the harrowing tales of war. His bravery and determination to survive were characteristic of his life.

Jim Charlesworth
Quarter Master Sergeant Royal Engineers

Jim Charlesworth, now resident in Smith's Row, Montacute, was nineteen years old when, in January 1940 he joined the Royal Engineers on a bitterly cold morning. Jim trained at Scarborough before embarking on the troopship SS *Scythia* in April 1940, sailing across the Atlantic, and joining another convoy bound for the Middle East.

The ship stopped at Durban for supplies and stores. Jim was here for six weeks and he remembers the hospitality he received from the South Africans. He was taken around and shown places of interest.

The soldiers had to report to the Military Police every forty eight hours while in Durban.

Next, the ship sailed from Durban up the Red Sea into the Suez Canal, and Jim landed at Suez in 1940.

Jim underwent more intensive training, using small arms, and engaged in mine clearance. It was at El Alamein, the turning point of the war in the desert, that Jim was fully engaged in mine clearance for the advance of tanks and heavy armour convoys onwards to Benghazi where Jim was recalled for further training.

In 1943 Jim sailed from Alexandria to Malta to deploy and help in drilling bore holes to find supplies of fresh drinking water for the islanders.

In November of that year, he returned to the Western Desert and remained there until January 1944. In 1944 Jim returned to the UK and took a well deserved month's leave before rejoining his unit at York. He undertook rigorous and intensive training before taking part in the "D Day" landings in France. Jim left Portsmouth and landed at Arromanches. His unit was responsible for assembling the Mulberry Harbour and making it safe for vehicles to get to the shore.

Jim remarked on the excellence of the Royal Air Force, flying constantly backwards and forward over the beaches to establish a bridgehead. Bitter fighting ensued to try to break out of the bocage, the heavily tree- and hedge- covered countryside which was an asset to the German army as cover for their soldiers and armoured vehicles.

After the breakout, the unit moved through France to Kiel and Hamburg, and Jim's unit was 60 miles from Berlin when the war ended.

Jim was eventually shipped back to England and demobbed from Doncaster in 1946.

Ivan Chick

Ivan Chick described his memories of Montacute and the Americans. He was born in Montacute at 14 South Street. His mother was killed in a road accident at Odcombe when he was three years old.

He was taken to Montacute School by his aunt. The school was run very smoothly. There were three teachers and Ivan said all the children could read and write before leaving school. Once a week the boys went to Stoke School for woodwork classes. The woodwork master was Tommy Lunn. If you misbehaved "he was more accurate with a piece of wood than Robin Hood."

On Bonfire Night preparations were made, with the men cutting gorse bushes and gathering hedge trimmings to bring to the Borough where there was a huge bonfire. All the doors and windows were boarded up because of the heat from the fire.

Another great night was Club Night when the men would walk through the streets with Bridgwater squibs. On arriving at the Borough they were greeted by the Anderton-Rowlands Fair with roundabouts and all the fun of the fair.

In Montacute House Lodge lived Mr Gold who was caretaker of the House. He also kept bees, and got Ivan interested in bee keeping. This led Ivan to obtain his first colony of bees in 1939. The neighbours were a bit dubious and wary of swarms of bees flying around but as time went by they calmed down when sugar was rationed and honey became available.

When the Americans arrived in Montacute Park, Ivan and Tony Trott got friendly with them and helped to get milk and run errands for them.

Ivan was very interested in his bees and timber being scarce in wartime he needed materials for his hives. Ivan obtained from the American soldiers a sheet of plywood and, after wondering how he was going to get it home, employed the help of Tony Trott to carry it.

So between them they carried it across the fields to Lowertown and passed it over the wall near the sheepwash, and proceeded up Lowertown to Hyde Road where Ivan was living. On the way up the road and struggling with the sheet, they came upon Mr Brimble the local policeman who asked them what they were doing. Ivan said, "we were given it to make a table-tennis table."

Mr Brimble allowed them on their way. A few weeks later Mr Brimble met Ivan and said, "I seen your table-tennis table turn into bee hives" – but nothing was done about it.

Montacute railway station was important during the war because the line connected Taunton with Yeovil. This allowed vital supplies to be transferred for military purposes which was especially vital in the build up to "D Day" because of the link between Yeovil and Weymouth where American forces embarked for Normandy.

When I spoke to the late Ken Rogers a couple of years ago, he remembered trains going through Montacute Station at night very slowly. He says, "they was probably carrying ammunition or explosives – all the carriages and trucks were blacked out." [Author]

Ivan also speaks of trains carrying American troops from Taunton to Yeovil. "As boys we would go to the station and watch them go by. As they were passing, the soldiers would throw out cigarettes and tobacco and chocolates and we would go along the track side and pick them up after the train had passed. I would keep them in my bedroom when living at Hyde Road so that I could have a crafty smoke."

"One particular day," Ivan said, "my father was out the front of the house when he called me and said to look at a German aeroplane flying over the railway station towards Yeovil followed by anti aircraft fire from nearby gun installations. I suddenly realised that I was stood on the doorstep next to my Father with a cigarette in my hand so I hastily departed up the garden but he never said anything. When I got married, at the reception my friend and I decided to go out and have a cigarette and my friend said, 'how long have you been smoking?' I replied, 'only recently !'

My father looked at us and said, 'No, he started when he was twelve', so he never forgot the time we stood on the step all those years ago!!"

"On V.E. Day 1945 my friends and I met in Montacute Borough, and decided to celebrate in our own way. Taking some empty bottles from the

King's Arms yard, we ventured towards Welhams Mill where they made cider. We got to the mill and filled our bottles with cider and wended our way back to the village, stopping on the way to have a good old drink out of the bottles. One of my friends, not content with this, picked a dandelion flower and took the bloom off and sucked the cider from the bottle up the stem of the dandelion all the way home. So that was our celebration of V.E. Day with, I expect, some sore heads from the cider."

Gunner Bertie Drayton
1118073
72nd Field Regiment
Royal Artillery

Bertie Drayton was living in South Street, Montacute, aged four, in the year 1911, the son of Herbert and Elizabeth Drayton.

Bertie grew up in Montacute and was described as a lively young man, prone to taking part in adventurous activities.

One particular adventure occurred while walking out with his friends in Montacute Park. Bertie always had an eye for the fruits of nature and while walking through the long grass, he suddenly dived to the ground, pulling out from underneath him a rabbit which had been hidden in the grass, and took it home for the pot.

Bertie also liked fighting and was often to be seen fighting with his friends in the Borough .

One bonfire night, Bertie was with one of his friends by the old post office (now known as The Chantry) which was in the corner of the Borough near the entrance drive to Montacute House. Bertie crept up behind P. C. Smart, the policeman, and let off a squib firework, with the result that he was chased through the village by the policeman.

When war came, Bertie was called to serve and joined the Royal Artillery, the 72nd Field Regiment. He was sent to the Middle East and while on embarkation leave, Bertie said to his friends that when the war was over he was going to join up with the Arabs.

Sadly, Bertie's wish never came true. He was killed on 30 May 1942 aged thirty-five, and is remembered with honour at the Knightsbridge War Cemetery, Acroma.

L.A.C. Wyndham Harold Drayton
1703260 Royal Air Force
Volunteer Reserve

Wyndham was born in Montacute at number 30 Townsend on 25 January 1923. He attended Montacute School and after leaving was employed at the Taunton & Thorne Glove Factory, as a warehouse man. Wyndham remained working here till war came when he joined the Home Guard in the village.

On 8 December 1941 Wyndham volunteered to join the Royal Air Force Volunteer Reserve at Salisbury, Wiltshire. He trained as an ACHU/T Wireless Operator with 3 Wing, A Squadron, 427 Unit.

In 1943 Wyndham was posted to India and served there till 1946. He continued his trade as a wireless operator; he was also employed in the officers' mess as a barman and to keep the mess records.

He remembers some good Christmases he had in India, especially with his mates. He

always remembered a mate of his, sounding the last post every evening at sunset.

After his service in India, Wyndham returned to the United Kingdom and was released from the RAF on 4 September 1946.

He was awarded the Defence Medal for his Home Guard service.

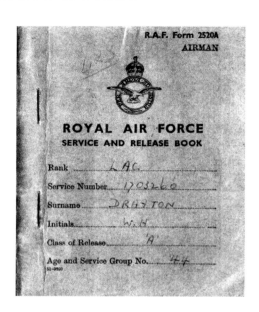

Mr and Mrs Drayton at their wedding.

John Dunston

John remembers the American forces in Montacute. He found them friendly. He recalled his mother helping with the laundry. His family was living at 19 Lower Hyde Road. There were two Americans who were especially friendly, Bill Morgan and Johnny Treminski. The washing was always brought down in a Willies Jeep and when it was ready, John said he would always have a ride back to Montacute House in the Jeep, but had to walk home.

On one particular occasion, John and a friend, Michael Gaylard, were standing on the corner of Bishopston near the King's Arms, when three American Sherman tanks came through the village.

John said, "As the tanks approached the corner the first tank slewed on its tracks and ripped down the garden wall of Captain Keep's property, opposite the church. The other two tanks just followed on – none of them stopped, they all carried on in the direction of Yeovil."

Restored Sherman tank at Weymouth.

John shows the repaired damage done by the Sherman tank.

Sergeant Pam Else
South African Air Force

Pam was born in Johannesburg, South Africa, in 1925. She attended school there and was fourteen when the war broke out in Europe. Pam joined the South African Air Force in 1943 when she was eighteen. Pam said that "families would have to do something to help the war effort."

Pam trained at Pretoria and took up duties as a meteorologist with the Air Force to assist with weather forecasts, plotting synoptic charts for daily forecasts. Various personnel were in different areas of South Africa taking air pressures and wind strengths and would then phone in or radio in to Headquarters where Pam co-ordinated information for the daily forecast.

It was during these duties that Pam discovered one man had phoned in the same report day after day, which was giving false information. This could have caused a very serious situation for operational aircraft – so action was taken to rectify the false information.

During Pam's service with the South African Air Force she was paid three shillings and sixpence a day.

Pam was discharged from the service in January 1946. She was awarded the South African Silver War Medal.

Pam's husband, Douglas, was born in Luton in 1921. He grew up in Luton and eventually worked for the de Havilland Aircraft Company at Hatfield as an aircraft electrician, helping to build aircraft.

When the war started, Douglas joined the Royal Air Force. He was selected for aircrew and did his flying training in Canada and America. He qualified as a navigator, flying in Mosquito fighter bombers. Douglas took part in a number of operational sorties.

Douglas and Pam were married in 1957 and eventually moved to Montacute in 1963.

Mr Bill Fall

Bill, together with his family, originated from London but on the 1 September 1939 all the children from his district were gathered together at a meeting point in the Walworth Road. They had a label with their name and address on tied to their coats and stood there with suitcases and gas masks slung over their shoulders.

There were loads of trams lined up in the road to take the children to Waterloo Station on what they thought was a practice run for the evacuation of all the children from London.

When they got off the trams there was a short walk to the station and there were lots of people lining the route, mainly women wearing pinnies and with tears streaming down their faces. One of them shouted , "Come on kids give us a song" and a teacher started up "It's a long way to Tipperary" and they all joined in.

The children boarded the train and a whistle blew and away they went, nobody knew where. After what seemed an endless journey the train stopped at Yeovil Town Station. The children climbed aboard buses that were to take them to their final destination which turned out to be Montacute church.

There were plenty of people bustling around organising where the children should be billeted. Bill's turn came and he went up past the recre-

Bill (on the right), Patrick and their sister Florence.

ation field and into Hyde Road, finally stopping at No 14. Bill's knock on the door was answered by a young man who looked as surprised as Bill felt. "Come in," he said, "and sit down. I'll fetch Mother." Bill sat down on the settee and after a few moments the young man came back with his mother. "Hello," she said, "I am Mrs Rogers and this is my son Ken and this is my daughter Ruth. What is your name?" He told her "Bill Fall," and was made very welcome.

Later on Bill was put to bed and next day met Mr Rogers who said, "Don't worry, son, you'll be alright."

On the 3 September at 11 a.m. Bill had to meet his teachers Mr Scott, Mr Gill and Mr Odham on the recreation field. Bill had been told that war had been declared so what Bill had thought had been a practice run on the evacuation was now reality. Montacute School was not big enough to take the London children as well as local children so they had to share half days. On rainy days the children had lessons in the church and on fine days they went for nature walks.

Bill's stay with Mr and Mrs Rogers was a happy one and they treated him just like one of the family. They made him write home every week and they used to laugh because every letter began, "Dear Mum and Dad thanks for the shilling and the comics," which he received every week.

For a while things were quiet and some of the children returned home to London.

In September 1940 the air raids were concentrated on the cities and Bill's mother and sister had some awful experiences so Bill's father sent them down to Montacute. The Rogers family kindly took them into their house to be with Bill. Not long after that, Bill's home in London was bombed so his Dad came down to Montacute too.

Arrangements were made for Bill's parents to stay with Mrs Rogers' sister in Chiselborough and shortly after they were able to get a thatched cottage in West Chinnock. Later the Co-op bought three houses in Bishopston, Montacute and luckily Bill's parents were allocated one.

Bill's mother took to country life like a duck to water. She joined the WI and the WVS and she and Bill's father did everything they could to help the war effort. But they also promised Bill's brother, Patrick, that the family would be together in London again when the war was over. Sadly, Bill's brother was killed in Burma and is commemorated on the Rangoon Memorial.

Private Patrick Henry Fall 6149336
Queen's Own Royal West Kent Regiment

Patrick Fall was the son of Frederick and Amelia Fall of Bishopston, Montacute. He was born in Southwark, London, in 1920. After leaving school in Southwark, Patrick worked for the Woolwich Arsenal in London. Patrick joined the Territorial Army, and when war was declared he was at camp in Lympne, Kent, with the Queen's Own Royal West Kent Regiment. During this period the Battalion was split up, some going to Tunbridge Wells and some to Axminster in Devon. While at these bases, the Battalions were brought up to strength with men, arms, and equipment.

In February 1940, the Battalion was inspected by King George at Lyme Regis and the soldiers realised that they were soon going into action. The Royal West Kents left England and landed in France in 1940, advancing into France and Belgium. Here they saw action. Due to heavy enemy opposition the Battalion withdrew but assisted in a rearguard action to enable the rest of the army to reach the coast and Dunkirk. It was here that the

Regiment was rescued and returned to England.

The Battalion went to Cowley Barracks, Oxford, and reformed, under-going intensive training and exercises.

In 1942 the Royal West Kents embarked on the troopship, *Laconia*, sailing from Liverpool with over four thousand troops. A convoy of some thirty vessels, together with the Royal Naval ship HMS *Nelson*, sailed for Africa. This was Patrick Fall's first tour with the 4th Battalion. He must have wondered about what he would encounter, and what it would be like to face battle.

The convoy reached Capetown safely. News filtered through of the fall of Tobruk in North Africa. Together with the rest of the Battalion, Patrick rested for a few days and took shore leave, appreciating the hospitality of the country. After resting, the Battalion's next port of call was Tewfic. After disembarking, they went to a transit camp, eventually joining the Division at Kataba.

In North Africa General Montgomery had taken command of the Eighth Army. Patrick Fall with his Battalion played their part in the Battle of El Alamein which was a crucial battle. The victory was the turning point of the war in the Allies' favour. After the Battle of El Alamein, the Royal West Kent Regiment was on the move again, this time to Burma. The journey took them through Palestine and Trans Jordan and into Iraq where they stayed for a while before sailing from the Persian Gulf to Bombay, India. On arrival in Bombay, the troops were greeted by a brass band.

They left Bombay and spent five days on a train to the middle of nowhere amongst scrubland and barren waste with the temperature around 114 degrees.

After resting and more training, the Battalion crossed the border into Burma where they were to encounter the hazards of the jungle, dense vegetation and swampy terrain. Another difficulty was replenishment of food, water, arms and ammunition.

With the Japanese forces advancing, the two armies were about to clash and clash they did, with intensive fighting and casualties. It was during the Battle of Kohima, 1944, that the Royal West Kents fought a brave and heroic stand against the Japanese forces. The 4th Battalion, to which Patrick Fall was attached, went into action with 500 men, holding back the enemy to keep the road to Diapur open, which enabled the British reinforcements to get into the battle area.

Some of the heaviest fighting took place around the Deputy Commissioner's bungalow and tennis court – this was the famous "Battle of the Tennis Court" where the opposing forces took to hand to hand fighting.

Relief came in April 1944 in the form of supporting British and Allied forces, together with artillery and Hurricane fighter-bombers of the Royal Air Force which pounded Japanese positions. By 13th May, Kohima was back under British control, but not without great loss of lives.

The Royal West Kents' 4th Battalion lost 61 killed, 13 missing and 125 wounded.

It was here, sadly, that Private Patrick Henry Fall was killed in the line of duty to the Queen's Own Royal West Kent Regiment on 13 April 1944. His name is inscribed with honour on the Rangoon Memorial. The epitaph on the memorial reads very appropriately:

> **"When you go home, tell them of us**
> **and say for their tomorrow we gave**
> **our today."**

Second Lieutenant Robert Michael Fenning

Robert Michael Fenning who lived at Lower Town, Montacute was born in Exeter in 1921 and educated in Exeter.

On 1 September 1939 a school friend, Dick Bishop, came around to Bob's house and said, "Why don't we join up in the Army?" Bob replied, "What a good idea!" and so they both cycled to Barrack Road, Exeter where LAA Battery Artillery was stationed. Both boys joined and rode home to tell their parents. Bob said that the news was not greeted with great enthusiasm but without condemnation.

The next day Bob reported to the barracks and was issued with a gunner's uniform. Shortly after that a number of reservists were needed to make up the battery strength and for some peculiar reason Bob was made a Lance Bombardier. He was put in charge of a squad of reservists and told to patrol the streets of Exeter; to make sure that no troops went into the pub just below the Guild Hall because it was a house of ill repute, and to make sure that no lower ranks went into the Clarence Hotel as it was reserved for officers!

In November 1939 the Battery was sent to France but as Bob was only eighteen years old, he was not allowed to go overseas and was posted to 84 London Transport HAA TA Regiment, and to a gun position in Finsbury Park. The unit was equipped with 3 ins guns which were a relic of the First World War. The fuses on the shells were all preset and had a protective cover on them to keep them dry. These turned out to be condoms and a notice went up on the Battery Notice Board to the effect that they all had a hole in the end and were not suitable for other purposes! As an eighteen-year old, Bob's education was proceeding rapidly!

In April 1940 Bob went before a War Office Selection Board and then to an OCTU at Shrivenham where after two months he was commissioned as a full blown 2nd Lieutenant and was ready to join a regiment. Bob was posted to 4th HAA Regiment, again stationed in North London, and joined 6th Battery which had the modern 3.7 inch guns. In those days there was no radar and the only help they had to try and put shells somewhere near the enemy aircraft, was to use the searchlight and sound locating equipment. As the sound locator had the bearing of the enemy aircraft and an estimate of the height, they then tried to plot the course of the aircraft and hopefully get the shells to burst somewhere near it. It was not very accurate but the civil population felt that at least something was being done! All of this went on during the siege of London, but as Bob's Battery was out to the north of the city it was not subject to any of the serious bombing.

In fact they were very close to Waltham Abbey which has a connection with the Montacute legend of the Black Cross.

Sometime in the spring of 1941 Bob volunteered to become a bomber pilot, he was not quite sure why! He had to go to Warrington for an interview and was accepted. Bob's regiment was then selected to be posted overseas and Bob was asked whether he wanted to be a pilot in the RAF or stay with 4th HAA Regiment. Very fortunately Bob chose to stay with the Regiment and that is probably why he is still here!

Bob was given forty-eight-hour embarkation leave and was then sent to Southend to get kitted up with all the paraphernalia for hot climates and then, by train, to Newport in South Wales. Bob embarked on the *Port Chalmers*, a ship which brought frozen meat from New Zealand. He did not know where he was going and his Commanding Officer had sealed orders which he was only allowed to open after twenty-four hours at sea. It was then learnt that the ship was going to Malta. The ship was carrying, as well as the troops, ammunition and fuel, which was not discovered until later!

There were six merchant ships in the convoy escorted by one battle ship HMS *Nelson*, one aircraft carrier, two cruisers and 24 destroyers. HMS *Nelson* left the convoy at Gibraltar. The convoy underwent a large number of attacks, shore shelling from Pantelliera, dive bombing, torpedoes and high level bombing. One destroyer was sunk, HMS *Fearless*. One merchant ship was hit in the forward hold but managed to reach Malta with the rest of the convoy, where Bob spent his first two nights in the barracks at Fort St Elmo overlooking the Grand Harbour.

Selection 1 from Bob Fennel in action on convoy to Malta.

On the second night Bob did a 'recce' to find out what was going on in Valetta and staggered back to bed only to be woken up by heavy gunfire. So he went out to the ramparts and, having come from London, looked up into the sky. There was nothing to be seen until it dawned on him that the firing was coming from seaward. There was an Italian E boat attack on the convoy moored in the Grand Harbour but none of them got through the defences so Bob was able to return back to bed! The next day the troop was deployed to gun positions in the south of the island in a village called Bubakra. It was just opposite a very small uninhabited island called Filfla, which Bob discovered was used by the Royal Air Force as a practice target for their low level attacks. The troop had four 3.7 ins HAA guns, a UB2 height finder and a Sperry predictor. There were two officers on the gun position, a chap called John Brain who was twenty-one and Bob who was twenty. They had been in the London blitz, but on a battery position of eight guns with the Battery commander in charge. Thank God that in Malta there were a number of experienced NCOs! Most days they were involved in firing barrages over the Grand Harbour or engaging enemy aircraft.

In one engagement Bob's gun crew were ordered to open fire on ME109 aircraft which were circling the island at 30,000 feet in order that the shell burst would point the way for Spitfires to intercept the enemy. Bob remembers one particular 109 dropping lower in height and his gun continuing to fire at this aircraft which took a hit from a shell burst with the fuse setting on the shell head smashing its engine block. The 109 made a crash landing on the island and personnel later dismantled the rest of the aircraft for intelligence purposes.

Selection 2 from Bob Fenning with the ME109 wreckage and Valetta.

When Bob had any time off he used to go along to Taquali aerodrome and cadge flights with Beaufighters and Wellingtons on their test flights after servicing. This was in early 1943 when the siege of Malta was really over. In the summer of 1943 Randolph Churchill came to the island to recruit two Squadrons for the 2nd SAS. Bob volunteered, was accepted and towards the end of the summer left Malta for Bizerta in North Africa where the 2nd SAS was based. He spent the first two nights on a bare hillside before being transported to Phillipville where the Regiment was based. Parachute training started very soon. There were no balloon jumps – thank heavens!

The training was to run down the back of a 3 tonner which was travelling at 15 mph, jump off, rotate through 180 degrees remaining upright, land and go into the forward roll. It seemed to work!! He then had forced marches, night time orienteering etc.

It seemed to him that every officer had a Jeep and when he asked how to get one, he was told to take a Jeep key to the American base and ask if they had a Jeep to fit it; to his considerable surprise this was successful.

Bob commanded H Squadron and waited somewhat apprehensively to go on an operation. Nothing much happened and he did a few ops in boats to try to get escaped P.O.W.'s out of Italy but that was a bit of a failure as most of them decided to wait for the 8th Army to advance through Italy.

As a matter of interest his Commanding Officer was Bill Stirling, brother of David Stirling who founded the "SAS" from the Long Range Desert Group who did so much good work in the Western Desert. His regiment consisted of a wide range of soldiers and the French squadrons had a number of men from the Foreign Legion, some of them being Germans.

Bob continued parachute training and persuaded the RAF Liaison officer to let him do a free fall from 5000 feet. Normally of course the chutes were opened when anyone jumped, by the rip cord handle being connected to a line inside the aircraft as the men queued up to jump. This would pull the rip cord as they jumped out and retain the cord to prevent tangles. On this occasion Bob had to count 1 to 10 very quickly and pull the handle himself on the way down!!

Unfortunately or perhaps fortunately, Bob damaged his right knee and was returned to his regiment and put on a ship from Algiers to Liverpool where he found 4th HAA Regiment was in the same convoy. The convoy did not have any escort as far as he can remember and he was scared stiff!

The regiment was then posted to the Orkneys which was not a good posting after five years in Malta!

Bob spent most of the time there putting barrages over Scapa Flow and then moved to Dover where he was involved in trying to shoot down the Flying Bombs and remained there until the end of the war in Europe.

Donald Philip Gaylard
Royal Navy

Philip joined the Navy at the age of sixteen-and-a-half years. He trained as a seaman and was based at Plymouth. A photograph follows showing Philip second from the right in the middle row, part of Hawk 15 Class St George 1941.

Philip joined the battleship HMS *Rodney* which must have been hugely exciting for a young seaman from Montacute. The next photograph is of the crew at Christmas 1942 which HMS *Rodney* spent at sea, their young faces showing that they were making the best of Christmas. Philip is in the first row, second from the right. The person first on the left in the front row is balancing a jar of military pickle on his head and the sailor in the middle looks as if he has a simulated Christmas cake on his head.

HMS *Rodney* was built by Cammell Laird, Birkenhead, launched in 1925 and completed in November 1927. With a displacement of 38,000 tons fully loaded, she was powered by two oil-fired geared turbines giving her a speed of 23.8 knots. The main armament consisted of 9 x 16 inch guns, 12 x 6 inch guns, and also included Pom-Pom guns and torpedoes. The crew complement was 1640.

Hawk 15 Class St George 1941.

L.G. Muggeridge.	W. J. Flower	E.P. Anderson.
H. A. Lax.	C. W. Franklin	D. McPherson(Ld.Boy)
R.B. Froud	H. J. Bridge	Geo. E. Heron. (L.P.O)
C.L. Broad	H. A. Hogarth	Mr. Coleman.(Gnr.)
J.B. Totton.	D. E. Gamblin(P.O.Boy)	F. Pitt-Palmer. (D.O)
C.E. Doyle	J. Macfarlane.	Ed. R. Cook (L.P.O)
A.G. King	N. Darby	D. G. Howard
R. Read.	D.P. Gaylard	F. Young.
B. Stenson.	R. J. Dixon	From Left to Right
BACK ROW	**MIDDLE ROW**	**FRONT ROW**

Personnel identification taken from the back of the photograph.

Christmas 1942 on HMS Rodney.

In 1942 HMS *Rodney* sailed with her crew including Seaman Philip to the Mediterranean ocean for naval operations and defence of convoys. HMS *Rodney* took her fair share of attacks from enemy aircraft and 'E' boats. She had a number of successes against enemy aircraft though she herself suffered minor damage. HMS *Rodney* returned to Plymouth for repairs and later rejoined the Fleet for convoy duties.

On 12 July 1943 HMS *Rodney*, with 1st Division, sailed to Malta where she anchored off the breakwater. This was the first visit of a British battle-ship since December 1940.

It was on this occasion that Philip met Gordon Geard who was serving with the RAMC in Gibraltar.

Apparently Gordon heard that Philip was aboard the HMS *Rodney* and arranged a meeting with him. It must have been a quite unique occasion when the two servicemen from Montacute met on HMS *Rodney*.

On 6 June 1944 HMS *Rodney* sailed for "SWORD" Beach during the Normandy landings, on arrival the ship was ordered back to Spithead.

On 7 June she returned to "JUNO" Beach and at 1830 hours opened fire on enemy forces driving the Canadian division back from Caen. The ship fired 132 X 16" shells and 99 X 6" shells.

On 12 August HMS *Rodney* took part in the bombardment of a gun battery on Alderney in the Channel Islands successfully damaging three out of four guns in the battery.

HMS *Rodney* returned to Portland and later to Plymouth and eventually Scapa Flow. While here, on the 29 November, she received the flag of C.inC. Home Fleet and remained in Scapa Flow until April 1945.

After the end of the war HMS *Rodney* was laid up at Rosyth and finally scrapped in 1948.

Philip Gaylard left the Royal Navy having attained the rank of Petty Officer.

Corporal Alfred Gordon Geard
Royal Artillery – Royal Army Medical Corps

On 16 April 1942, Gordon, a leather cutter living in Montacute, was called up for service and had to report to Lufton Camp, Yeovil, to be enlisted in the Light Anti Aircraft Royal Artillery. He remembers his square bashing and being shouted at and called all sorts of things. "I had five weeks of training at Lufton Camp and was then marched to Pen Mill Station and put on a train to Birkenhead, Cheshire."

From there, Gordon was sent to a Battery at New Brighton, and took part in guarding a radar station at Speke. He returned to Birkenhead for three weeks' training on Bofors guns.

In July 1942, while at Birkenhead, the unit was told that Rommel had pushed our troops back to the gates of Cairo, and if the Germans got through to Egypt and seized the Suez Canal, they would go on to take India.

"We knew we were going overseas, so I came home on embarkation leave in August 1942. On return from leave the unit boarded a train and travelled to Greenock on the river Clyde. We joined the ship *Llanstephan Castle* where we were issued with tropical kit. The rumour was that we were going to Freetown on the west coast of Africa.

"The journey took us toward South America and then we zig-zagged back to Gibraltar. This was done to protect us from U boats."

Gordon said he was violently sea sick and ate just dry bread.

"After three days at sea, we were glad to get off the ship at Gibraltar. Gathering our kit, we were marched to Europa Point. Our billets were just a tunnel in the rock. The beds had no mattresses and each soldier was issued with three blankets. Later we were transferred to better accommodation at Windmill Hill Barracks."

Gordon and his gun crew had regular drill on gunnery. Practice entailed firing at a canvas tubular target (Drogue) towed some distance behind one of our aircraft. He said that they got quite good at hitting it with shell fire.

One day he was sent to have a medical and discovered that his left eye was not working properly. Consequently Gordon was taken off gun sighting and transferred to cook house duties which consisted of peeling spuds and scrubbing floors. He said this nearly drove him mad with boredom.

Gordon applied for a transfer to the Royal Army Medical Corps, and was duly accepted and transferred to the Military Hospital. Here he settled and flourished. Working hard, he gained numerous qualifications and was liked by staff and patients. Besides British and allied soldiers, Gordon also treated wounded German soldiers and prisoners.

He remembers one particular soldier named Roerig who was only seventeen years old. He was suffering from perforated intestines and Gordon felt sorry for him. While Roerig was receiving treatment he had to have an armed guard by his bedside at all times. Gordon thought this was ridiculous so the guard was removed, and he nursed the young man back to health.

Gordon left Gibraltar to return to England in 1946. Landing at Tilbury Docks, he boarded a train to London and eventually was demobbed at Aldershot, with a month's pay.

He returned to his trade as a glove cutter.

John Frederick Guppy (Jack)
1913 – 1969

Jack was well known in Montacute and in the neighbouring villages as a family butcher at 22 Bishopston, Montacute. His shop, where he served meats and produce, was always busy.

He married Dorothy Chaffey in 1939, and a year later was called up to serve in the Royal Artillery, serving in India for five years. His duties included cooking for the messes.

Jack Guppy, Butcher, Montacute.

He returned safely to England after the war years and met Dorothy quite unexpectedly near the Yeovil Town railway station, quite a reunion after five years apart. Jack and his wife continued to run the village butcher shop successfully together. Dorothy had run the shop on her own all through the war and rationing.

During his years in Montacute, he was Treasurer of the Montacute Provident and Mutual Benefit Society, and a member of Montacute Working Men's Club. He was also a Special Constable.

In 1946 their daughter Jacqueline was born. Jacqueline married Dave Fox and they still live in Montacute.

Sadly, Jack became ill and died in August 1969 of Hodgkin's Disease at the age of fifty six.

I remember Jack well. I bought my first shotgun from him for six pounds and used it for many years.[Author]

The shop front is still in existence in Bishopston but is now a private home.

Humphrey Hamlin

Humphrey was born to parents Grace and Tim Hamlin, 10 Bishopston, Montacute, in 1932 He attended Montacute School from 1937, the Headmaster being Mr Fane, and here he gained a scholarship to Yeovil Grammar School where he started in 1942 at eleven years old.

On his way to school in Yeovil one day, the bus was reaching Houndstone Corner when a German Messerschmitt 109 Fighter zoomed low overhead flying south. With great excitement all the boys went to the side windows of the bus and gazed in amazement. At the same time the Bofors gun which was positioned near Alvington opened fire on the aircraft. It didn't score any hits, however, and the aircraft disappeared from sight. It was also while Humphrey was at Yeovil School that a German Dornier bomber flew across Yeovil, very near the school heading north and Humphrey, with other boys, remarked how low it was. "So low," he said, "that you could see the pilot and aircrew."

Humphrey remembers the bombing of Houndstone Camp when soldiers were killed, he said, "We took shelter under the table in the house while the attack happened." He also recalls the terrible raids on Bristol, of aircraft passing overhead with the drone of the German desynchronized engines. The raids resulted in many Bristolians being killed and buildings being damaged or destroyed. Humphrey remarked that you could look towards Bristol and see the glow in the sky of the city in flames.

Humphrey also spoke of the bomb dropped near Montacute Station. He remembers going down Station Hill and seeing the crater in the field.

He also recalls going out with other boys during wartime collecting bits and pieces, and going up to Ham Hill near the old lime kiln where the Americans had a firing range. Here they picked up spent cartridge cases and dug out old bullets from the banks and fitted them together. The photograph on the right shows American 30.06 cartridges in the clip and a 45 A.C.P. cartridge either side of the clip.

Humphrey's father, Mr Tim Hamlin, played his part in the war effort by joining the Auxiliary Fire Service, whose headquarters were at Martock. Humphrey says that Montacute had a portable pump, and Tim and his colleagues used to practice fire drill by going down to the sheep wash in Lower Town and starting up the pump which was powered by a petrol fuelled engine. They used the water hoses for fire practice but the pump was used sparingly because of the shortage of petrol and Humphrey said that instead of using the pump for fire practice, to conserve petrol the fireman would make hissing noises to simulate the water leaving the hoses.

Humphrey's father Tim is 2nd row from the top and 5th from the left.

Humphrey's father's CDCW service insignia.

Humphrey's father remembers seeing the huge stock piles of petrol jerry cans which the Americans had placed along the track leading to Brympton House. If these had been bombed, the firemen would certainly have needed more than a portable pump.

Humphrey picked up a leaflet dropped over Montacute by German aircraft informing the British of the might of the German Armed Forces and their intentions in the event of invasion towards this country. In spite of these threats our country survived.

Keith Hann

Keith's earliest recollection of the Second World War was seeing his father leave home to "join up". Keith was just four years old. The date was 17 July 1941. Keith and his mother saw his father off to war from Montacute Station.

The new recruits did their basic training before being sent to their new camps in various parts of the country. Keith's father was sent to Liverpool to join the Pioneer Corps (hence his support for Liverpool Football Club).

He spent some time fire fighting in the docks.

Keith's father rose to the rank of Regimental Sergeant Major. Prior to his demobilisation in June 1946, he was offered a commission to stay on in the Army but declined. The latter part of his war service was spent in and around the London area working with his troops to help clear large areas following the devastation from the awful bombing raids that occurred over London. It was here that he, like many, experienced the V-bombs or "doodlebugs."

Keith's father was a very good cricketer, being a fast bowler. Before the war, Montacute had a very good cricket team and travelled all over Somerset to play. There was one occasion when Montacute were playing Watchet who had an extremely good opening batsman by the name of Harold Gimblett. He was on the verge of joining Somerset as a professional. Keith's father, however, opened up the bowling and bowled Harold Gimblett out first ball. As he walked past Keith's father, he said, "Well bowled, William! When I come to Montacute, I will repay the compliment."

Well, later that season, at Montacute, Harold opened the innings for Watchet and Keith's father opened the bowling for Montacute (the cricket pitch in those days was in the park, with Odcombe people seated on one side of the ground and Montacute folk on the other, never the twain shall meet). Harold dispatched Keith's father for six sixes in his first over, after which he walked down the wicket, shook William's hand and said, "Now, William, we're quits." Keith's father repaid that feat by bowling him out in his next over. Harold Gimblett went on to play for Somerset and England for many years after the war ended.

During Keith's father's time in and around the London area, he was chosen to play cricket for the Army side which included the England cricketers Cyril Washbrook and Jack Ikin (of Lancashire) and Hedley Verity (of Yorkshire). Keith's father was selected to play many times with them.

With his father away from home, his mother would make him a "mint" sweet which was based on a sweet known as a "Nuttall's Minto". She would take some powdered milk (which was issued by the Government and used to come in large tins), mix up a dough, add some peppermint essence and roll the mixture into little balls. Once they hardened, they were just like the real thing and she would send some off to his father.

On occasions when his father came home on leave, he would bring Keith wooden toys. His army pal, Alex McCarthy, whose home was in Scotland, spent his spare time making these toys. There was one occasion when William brought home a large wooden bus which Keith could sit on and ride up and down the garden path. Then there was a wooden train set with carriages to attach to the engine.

Just before the war ended, Alex came home with Keith's father for a short leave before they were demobilised. Alex introduced Keith to Natural History, in particular British butterflies. They would walk to Ham Hill together and Alex would identify and explain the differences in habitats. Before he went home to Scotland, Alex gave Keith a book of British butterflies which is still in his bookcase.

Keith started school between 1941-2. The Headmistress was Miss Bryant, and the other teachers were Miss Winchester and Mrs Whittle. Despite the worries of war, school was generally quite a happy time for Keith.

When the enemy were flying over to bomb cities such as Bristol or cities in the Midlands, they made St Michael's Hill and Hedgecock Hill their flight landmarks. When this happened, the teachers would make the children shelter underneath the big metal and wooden desks. They could look up through the big glass windows and watch the bombers and fighter aircraft flying overhead. At times they could see the pilots and other crew members which Keith found very frightening.

There were barrage balloons aloft over Icicle Barn, tethered to the ground, and some artillery was in position.

There were occasions when the Germans would jettison unused bombs on their return flights home. On one occasion, they dropped their bombs near Stoke Secondary Modern School (this was before the authorities changed the name to Stanchester School). They believed the school to be a hospital. Glass was shattered in people's homes but thankfully there were no injuries.

One bomb fell in the field near to Montacute railway station. Keith can remember going to see the large crater and the shrapnel holes in the metal bars of the cattle pens at the railway station goods yard.

The radio played an important part during the war. Keith's mother would listen to the news broadcasts which kept the nation up to date with the latest situations around the world. He remembers Winston Churchill giving his many speeches during these dark and difficult days. At times, they would also hear propaganda broadcasts from

Germany. Their broadcaster was William Joyce, known as Lord Haw Haw an American-born British traitor. There was one broadcast in particular when he announced that the Luftwaffe had successfully bombed the "port" of Milborne Port, and on another occasion he announced that the Luftwaffe had bombed Bagnel Harbour [Bagnel Farm was within the parish boundary of Montacute until 1955].

The American Army arrived in the village towards the latter part of the war. There was a large military presence. This occurred prior to the "D-Day" Landings in early 1944. It created great excitement among all the children, who didn't know how serious the implications of this were.

With other young children, Keith would gather around their Jeeps and big "International" lorries and say, "any gum, chum?" This was the very first time that Keith had experienced chewing gum and American candy. The soldiers were a very carefree and friendly bunch. The big cultural shock was of course to see Afro-American men. As a young child, this was something Keith had only experienced through books, and coming face to face with these soldiers was a strange experience, but they too, were a very friendly, good humoured bunch of mostly young men. On the odd occasion, they would take youngsters for short rides in their Jeeps, which the children thought was great fun.

Keith's family have always worshipped at St Catherine's church [his ancestors are recorded as having lived in Montacute from around 1605], and continue to do so today. Keith has been a member of the Parochial Church Council for over fifty years. He is the current church treasurer (nineteen years to date) and Lay Chairman of the Ivelchester Deanery. His great grandfather, and father, all sang in the church choir, and other family members were bell ringers. His uncle, Herbert Hann, was Captain of the "bells" for many years.

Keith started Sunday School at two and a half years old. He was taken by older children to church on Sunday afternoons at 2.15 p.m. His first teacher was Miss Grace Welch who was also the church organist. Other teachers were Miss Mead, Mrs Langdon and Reverend Richard Beechey. Miss Mildred Geard was another Sunday School teacher. At some point during the war years, she went to work in a hospital in Bath. Mildred returned to Montacute after the war ended, where she taught at St Catherine's for many years. In those days, over 100 children attended Sunday School each Sunday.

Keith's grandfather, Rowland Hann, was a monumental stone mason by trade but during the war period he was also an Air Raid Warden, with the little metal plaque fixed on his front door. His area in Montacute was Hyde Road, Lower Town and St Michael's View. After completing a full day's work at the monumental masons' firm, "Appleby & Childs" in Yeovil, Rowland would come home for his meal and then go on duty as an Air Raid Warden, checking that all curtains were drawn at night and no lights were visible for the enemy to see. He was also responsible for keeping an eye open for strangers moving into the area. There was a slogan about avoiding loose talk in the company of strangers, and being on your guard at all times.

Keith's uncle, Bill Trotman, had been living with Keith's mother and father (due to Bill's mother dying at a relatively young age), prior to the commencement of the Second World War. Like many men, he was "called up" to serve his country although his eyesight was very poor. He was sent to join the Somerset Light Infantry, transferring at some point to the Durham Light Infantry. Keith remembers Bill coming home on embarkation leave in 1944 just before the invasion of France. Bill was killed in battle near Caen on 18 June 1944, aged thirty-six years. He is buried at the British War Cemetery at Bayeux in France.

At times during bombing raids on Yeovil, it was possible to hear the bombs exploding and also see the flares light up the skies. The Germans had knowledge of the Westland Aircraft Factory and the large military presence at Houndstone. Because of this information, the whole area was a regular target for bombing raids. These sites were attacked many times until the Luftwaffe was defeated.

During the war period and well into peacetime, food was rationed, which meant that there was never an abundance of food.

People who lived in the countryside could, if they had a garden, provide extra food for their families. There was a famous Government slogan – "Dig for Victory"; a small book was published which encouraged people to grow some of their own food.

Many families were evacuated from the big cities and were sent to the countryside where it was considered to be safer. A number of these families came to stay in the village, with their children attending the local schools. Keith's mother had someone called Rose Gatland staying with her. She came from Market Harborough in Leicestershire and her husband, Charlie, was at some time stationed at Houndstone Camp. Keith and his mother remained friends with the Gatland family until Rose died several years ago. Keith remembers also the Bolton family who stayed in Townsend, the Carswell family who lived in the Vicarage annexe, and the Webb family who came to live in Hyde Road. Many of these families never returned to their original homes.

After the war ended, the Bolton family remained in the area [in fact Charlie Bolton played football for Montacute for many years], as did the Carswell family who went to live in Yeovil. Keith knew Douglas Carswell quite well and they often met through playing football and cricket for their respective schools. Harold Webb and his mother returned to Camberwell at the end of the war.

Prior to the beginning of the Second World War, Keith's father rented an area of land (now known as Lower Hyde Road) from the local authority. He used the land to grow vegetables and keep chickens. At various times during his army service he would be given special leave to come home and harvest the crops.

Families had air raid shelters known as Anderson shelters. They were built on this piece of ground to help protect families from air raids. Large areas of the ground were dug out and then a strong, steel cover was placed over the hole. The inside of the shelter was usually lined with wood and made comfortable with seats that could be used as beds. When the air raid siren went off, families would gather up some warm clothes, bedding and food and make for the shelters. They would stay there until the "all clear" siren sounded and would then return to their homes.

After the war ended, the local authority used this land to provide homes for the demobbed soldiers and their families. Homes that were made from pre-assembled parts, known as "Pre-Fabs", were built as a cheap way to provide housing.

When the war finally ended, the village children watched as literally dozens of colourful coaches full of ex-servicemen drove through the village on their return to this country. The children, whose fathers had been away for nearly six years, couldn't wait for them to come home. Keith's father finally returned in June 1946.

It was then a time of adjustment for everyone, getting back into the flow of family life, and for some of the ex-service men it was to be extremely difficult.

Shirley Hann

Shirley Hann speaks of the Americans when they took over the Baptist school room for accommodation. Shirley, with the other children, would go past the chapel gate, just to hear the sentry on guard challenge – "Halt, who goes there?" She also remembers the Nissen huts in Montacute Park stretching from Montacute House to the Old Mill. Shirley told me of the name carved on the large tree near the entrance to the shop of the House, and the name etched in the stonework going into the old kitchen doorway. [Page 29].

Besides the Americans, there was the 226 Royal Artillery Regiment from Brighton and a Yorkshire regiment in the Park in 1943.

Shirley remembers the long hot summer days with picnics on Ham Hill and in the Park of Montacute House. Her schooldays were happy, but she says "there were scary times for us younger ones when identity cards and gas masks were handed out and we were told why we needed them."

She also said, "woe betide anyone who left their gas masks at home; we had to go back and fetch them. When the air raid siren went, we had to go to the cloakroom and collect our coconut mats and lie down on the floor until the danger had passed.

"I remember large convoys going through Montacute, which included lorries, tanks and artillery guns."

Edward Inglett
Royal Navy

Edward was born in Montacute, attending Montacute School. At the age of fourteen he went to work in Ricketts' Glove Factory, Yeovil.

In 1939, at eighteen years old, Edward volunteered to join the Royal Navy and after training was sent to the Aircraft Carrier, *Ark Royal*, on which he saw action in the Mediterranean.

On 10 November *Ark Royal* and her escort sailed for Malta to deliver 37 Hurricanes which would fly ashore to the airfield when *Ark Royal* was close enough. The aircraft carrier reached Malta safely but on her return voyage to Gibraltar, she was torpedoed by the newly arrived U-81 submarine. Although the carrier was badly damaged, she tried to reach

Gibraltar, with the aid of sea going tugs. *Ark Royal's* boilers were relit and the lost steam raised again to power her pumps and engines.

On 14 November, twelve hours after being hit, fire started in the engine room. The fire put the *Ark Royal's* pumps out of action and the carrier's initial list got much worse. At about 0600 hours the *Ark Royal* capsized and sank. The crew, including Edward, abandoned ship and were later picked up. Edward was later retrained and sent to HMS *Jaguar*, a destroyer, still operating in the Mediterranean on escort and patrol duties.

Sadly, HMS *Jaguar* was torpedoed and Edward lost his life. A Petty Officer visiting the family in Montacute, said he remembered Edward swimming away from the stricken ship and that was the last he saw of him.

Later the family received a telegram confirming that Edward was lost at sea. Edward's name is engraved on the Plymouth Naval Memorial.

Mrs Joyce Monaghan (née Osborne)

Mrs Monaghan lived in South Street, Montacute, during the war.

She said, "war sharpened everyone. The village was excited when the Americans arrived at Montacute."

Some of the Americans were billeted in Montacute Baptist church school room. Joyce said, "there was a very young soldier with bright blue eyes, always gazing out of the window." She added – "probably thinking of home, looking out on the prairies of Texas." These soldiers were only eighteen to twenty years old.

Joyce also remembers the dances held at the Working Men's Club in Bishopston. The Americans would help out with the refreshments as food was rationed – in particular hot dogs. The Afro-American soldiers preferred jam on the sausage in their bread rolls.

Joyce befriended one particular soldier whose name was Wilfred Wavering. They remained friends while Wilfred was in Montacute and on the approach to "D Day" Joyce saw Wilfred off on a train from Pen Mill Station and her last memory was of him waving till the train was out of sight. That was the last time she saw or heard of him.

LACW Vi Myram
Women's Royal Air Force

Vi (short for Violet but she preferred to be called Vi) was born at Mutford, Suffolk but lived and grew up on the Isle of Wight where she also attended school.

During her teenage years, she worked for Pickford's Removal Company as an office administrator at Cowes but later worked for the Isle of Wight's Agricultural War Committee.

On reaching the age of eighteen Vi joined the WRAF and her first posting was to Wilmslow, Cheshire where she did her basic training (including drill and square bashing) and later trained as a clerk.

In 1941 Vi was posted to Barnwood, Gloucestershire to the Records Office with about 5000 other personnel.

Vi's next posting was to Ford in Sussex where the airfield was operating Hurricanes and Spitfires. While at Ford, Vi, as well as carrying out her clerical duties, helped with the refreshment of aircrew such as pilots who had been on operations or patrols. She served the men with food and drinks before their next sortie. Vi stayed at Ford until 1944 and then returned to the Records Office in Gloucestershire.

Vi met her husband, Robert, on the Isle of Wight where he was involved in building warships. Robert trained as a pilot in South Africa and reached the rank of Flying Officer. On completion of his training he returned to the United Kingdom and was attached to 802 Naval Air Squadron where he flew Hurricanes and Spitfires. His main base was HMS *Dipper* at Henstridge and he also operated from HMS *Heron*, Yeovilton

Vi came out of the Women's Royal Air Force at the end of 1944 and returned to the Isle of Wight at Wootton.

At the end of the war, Vi and Robert had a business at Newbury and also lived at Huntingdon before moving to Montacute in 1992 to a house in the Borough , which had been used for military administration during the war.

Edwin George Northam
Trooper 7905315
48 Royal Tank Regiment RAC

Edwin Northam, brother of Charles, joined the Royal Tank Regiment and after training left for North Africa.

On 15 March 1943, Edwin's ship left, in convoy, at 5 a.m. from Gourock Bay on the Clyde near Glasgow. It was a rough passage and most of the troops were seasick. While sailing through the Mediterranean, the convoy was attacked by Italian aircraft. These aircraft were carrying torpedoes and one ship was hit.

The convoy arrived at Bone, its destination, at 6 p.m. on 25 March. The troops disembarked and marched 8 miles to No 4 Transit Camp.

While in Tunisia, the Battalion formed part of the 21st Tank Brigade of the British First Army, C Squadron, and went into action in May with the support of an infantry battalion.

The attack was successful. After fighting ceased in Tunisia, the Battalion was withdrawn to the area around Bone, where they stayed for almost a year.

On 30 April 1944 the Battalion embarked for Italy. Tanks and lorries landed at Taranto, including Trooper Northam.

On 1 August, the Battalion was placed under the command of the 1st Canadian Infantry Division and C Squadron went into action in September. They saw the fiercest fighting of the Italian Campaign, suffering heavy casualties.

On 13 December, the Battalion was with the 2nd New Zealand Division and C Squadron supported the 43 Ghurkha Brigade.

For the final offensive in Italy in April 1945, the Battalion was placed under the command of the 8th Indian Division and together captured Venice. The Germans surrendered on 2 May 1945.

The Battalion moved to Rimini and was billeted in seaside hotels. Leave was granted to Edwin and he went to the UK to see his new baby for the first time.

On his return to Italy tragedy struck. Edwin was killed in a road accident on 7 September 1945. He is buried with honours in the Ancona War Cemetery, Rimini, Italy.

Edwin was aged twenty-eight years.

Douglas Pilton
Royal Navy

Douglas (Doug) Pilton was born in Montacute in 1926, one of three brothers, and attended Montacute School.

When war came, Doug joined the Royal Navy and enlisted at HMS *Drake*, Plymouth, where he did his basic training. After training, he was posted to various ships including sloops and destroyers – one of these ships was HMS *The Wild Goose* a Black Swan class sloop.

Doug and his shipmates took part in the "Battle of the Atlantic" where German "U" boats were sinking our supply convoys. These submarines originally hunted singly but their tactics changed to hunting in groups, known as Wolf Packs.

Priority orders came through for all our efforts to be concentrated on destroying these German submarines to stop the loss of shipping.

During May of 1943 the Allies were still suffering great losses but with new technology and improved equipment the tide was turned in their favour. Large numbers of "U" boats were destroyed allowing important convoys to get through.

It was an important phase of the war and Doug's ship accounted for two submarines, with Doug assisting in the dropping of depth charges. He said, "We picked up four survivors of one crew and twenty three from another crew."

On returning to port, Doug was given a weekend leave and returned to Montacute to see his mother and told her about the sinking of the "U" boats, saying, "You would not have heard this on the BBC because of censorship."

Doug's next posting was escorting ships of the Russian convoys, one of the most dangerous missions of the war at sea. Doug remarked on the intense cold of the ice-bound waters and said he was chipping off the ice from the ships equipment and gun turrets to keep it all working." On his last voyage to Russia the ship got so far, when something went wrong with its equipment and had to return to port. Fate had lent her hand because that particular convoy was nearly wiped out by enemy action.

After the Russian convoys, Doug was posted to South Africa and there he remained until the end of the war. It was while Doug was serving in South Africa that he sustained an injury to his hand and reported sick. When he was fit, he was due some leave. He had to report to his Commanding Officer for him to sanction Doug's leave. Normally nobody ever got leave longer than a weekend but Doug's luck was in again. The Officer asked him where he lived and when Doug said, "Montacute, Somerset", the Officer replied, "I have had some wonderful times in Montacute House at parties and dancing." Doug remarked, "he must have come from a wealthy family to have been invited to the House on numerous occasions." The Officer gave Doug seven days' leave and told him, "it is a lovely village to spend your leave in, go home and enjoy it." Doug's Petty Officer could not believe he had been given seven days leave.

Doug was released from the Navy at the end of 1945 and returned to Montacute.

Norman Pilton

Norman describes his boyhood in Montacute with the Americans. Norman was living in Back Lane, near Rex Drayton's farm in 1943.

One of his first jobs in the early morning was to help deliver milk from the farm with Mildred and Vera Drayton, before going to school.

Norman got friendly with the American soldiers and he used to run errands for them. He told me that the Nissen huts for the accommodation of the soldiers were on the East Front of Montacute House.

Norman said one of the soldiers, Herby Bowser, played the piano and also played in a band in Chicago.

When the soldiers left the Park, Norman was given badminton racquets, shuttlecocks, and models of German, American and Allied aeroplanes which

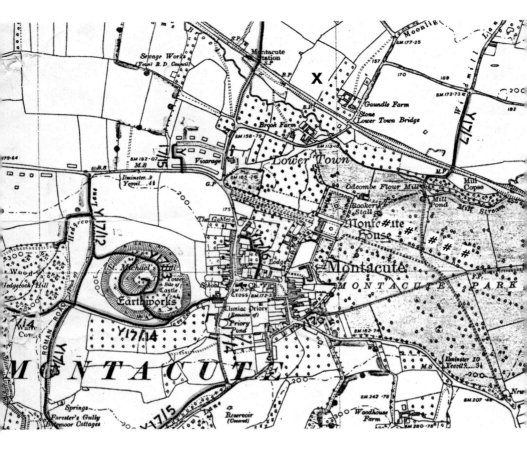

KEY :-- **X** SITE OF BOMB EXPLOSION, NEAR MONTACUTE STATION

AMERICAN FORCES NISSEN HUTS DURING OCCUPATION

the Americans had used for identification training purposes. At the time, the pastor at Montacute chapel was William Osborne, and, on hearing that Norman had aircraft models, he confiscated them saying they were classified material; Norman never got them back.

Norman also remarked on the large number of tracked vehicles and lorries passing, in convoy, through the village in the build up to "D Day".

William George Purdy (Bill) 1927-2013
Royal Navy

Bill was born in London at Lambeth in 1927 and attended school there, leaving school at twelve years of age. He was evacuated to South Petherton, Somerset.

He joined the Royal Navy on 24 October 1944 at HMS *Royal Arthur*, Corsham, Wiltshire. Here he did his Naval general training until 16 January 1945, Bill was then posted to HMS *Drake*, Devonport on 17 January, training as a stoker (an engine room rating) and this he completed on 14 May 1946.

After Bill's training he was posted to HMS *St Angelo* shore establishment in Valletta, Malta.

Bill's first ship was HMS *Coquette* (J350), an Algerian class fleet minesweeper. HMS *Coquette* was built in a Canadian shipyard.

Her original name was going to be HMS *Bowmanville* but she was launched as HMS *Coquette* in 1943.

The ship was part of a flotilla which served in the Far East as part of the Pacific Fleet before being sent to the Mediterranean to carry out minesweeping off the North African coast at Bizerta and also around Malta. HMS *Coquette* eventually returned to the United Kingdom.

In 1947 Bill returned to HMS *Drake* before being released from service on 12 January 1948.

Bob Reynolds RASC Montacute
and Gwyneth (Min) Trott
Women's Army Corps 1939 - 1945

Bob Reynolds from Hull, Yorkshire, was born in 1920. He joined the Royal Army Service Corps at seventeen years of age and served throughout the war.

It was while in the Army that he met his wife, Gwyneth Trott from Stoke sub Hamdon. She was serving in the Women's Royal Army Corps and they met at Blackburn, Lancashire where they were later married. Gwyneth left the service when Sheila, their eldest child, was born in 1943. Later, they had son, David, and another daughter, Rosemary.

NEWSPAPER REPORT:

Brothers Meet in Italy

After four years, the two sons, Fred and Tom, of Mr & Mrs A. Trott of 5 East Stoke, Stoke sub Hamdon have met in Italy. Fred, who is in the infantry, served in Northern Ireland for two years, returned to England for a few months and then went to Italy where he landed seven weeks ago.

Tom, a driver in the Royal Artillery, has been in the Middle East since 1941, and went right through the North African campaign.

He also landed in Italy seven weeks ago. On the same day as their meeting, the two brothers also met their brother-in-law, Private R. Reynolds, who has been in the Middle East for two years.

Bob and Gwyneth settled in Montacute from where Bob was called up again to serve in the Korean War.

Gerald (Jim) Shoemark
Royal Engineers

Jim was born in Montacute on 13 June 1919. His parents were Arthur and Ann Shoemark. Jim had one sister, Norah, two brothers, Basil and Donald, three stepbrothers, George, Herbert and William, and one stepsister, Mona.

Jim attended Montacute School and was later apprenticed to learn carpentry and joinery with Bartlett's of Yeovil.

At the outbreak of war, Jim enlisted in the Royal Engineers at Clacton-on-Sea on 29 January 1940. After basic training, Jim was given embarkation leave. He was sent to France on 16 March 1940 to be part of the British Expeditionary Force.

With the advance of the German army, the B.E.F. was forced to retreat further into France, being surrounded and cut off and driven onto the beaches of Dunkirk. It was here that "Operation Dynamo" took place, headed by Admiral Ramsay. This involved the evacuation of troops from the beaches with the aid of small ships, mostly civilian, taking the troops from the beach to the larger ships.

These small craft, of which there were many, some still in use, are now fondly remembered as "The Dunkirk Little Ships", and have their own organisation keeping the spirit alive. Over 330,000 men were rescued and taken back to England. Jim was picked up at St Malo on 19 June 1940 and returned to England.

He retrained and after further embarkation leave, was posted to India, and later to Burma in 1942. The Royal Engineers had an arduous task in the jungles of Burma, constructing jungle trackways for vehicles, to allow supplies to reach the troops. Jim stayed in Burma till the end of the war in Europe and the defeat of Japan. He left the Royal Engineers with the rank of Regimental Sergeant Major.

After the war, Jim returned to his profession of carpenter and joiner and to management in the construction industry. Working with his brothers Basil and Donald, the business came to be known as Shoemark Builders, Montacute. Jim also worked for Coombe's Builders, Ilminster, and eventually returned to Bartlett's of Yeovil until he retired.

Jim passed away on 25 October 2012.

I always had respect for Jim for although he left Montacute and went to live in Stoke sub Hamdon, he always attended Remembrance Services at St Catherine's church in Montacute. [Author]

Cpl Stanley Stagg
RAOC

Stan Stagg started his wartime life in the reserved occupation of building government specific works such as pillboxes for machine gun emplacements and air raid shelters etc. while employed by Pippard and Perry, builders of Yeovil. He recalls while working near Pen Mill Station in 1940, witnessing large formations of German aircraft apparently heading for Bristol to bomb the city.

Stan also worked at Filton, Bristol, carrying out essential work near the airfield. While working at Bristol several men were killed by enemy bombing. Leaving Bristol, Stan went to work at Henstridge Airfield to build bomb proof blast walls.

At the age of twenty years Stan was called up for military service. After his training he joined RAOC Regiment and eventually landed in France in 1944, four days after "D Day".

He described the slow progress through the countryside caused by the German defence positions, where there were pockets of German resistance. He slept under lorries or in ditches at night to try to gain some shelter from shelling and small arms fire.

Stan remembers crawling up a bank together with his mate, and looking down into a valley which contained German vehicles and tanks. While they were surveying the valley a flight of Hawker Typhoon fighter bombers appeared and started to strafe and fire rockets into the column of vehicles which set them alight. They beat a hasty retreat back to their unit.

Stan's unit then moved forward up the valley and made progress, advancing into Belgium and Germany.

While Stan was in Germany he played football for the Regiment and was asked to stay on after the war finished in Europe but he decided not to having served his time. Stan married Dorothy Masters in May 1945 in Montacute Baptist church. He was demobbed in 1946.

Cpl Stanley Stagg winter 1944.

Stan & Dorothy's wedding in May 1945 with (left to right) *Stan Samford, Stella Axe, Stan & Dorothy, Iris Masters (sister of the bride) and Jack Masters (brother).*

Henry (Harry) Tresidder
Army No. 7952529
Gunner – Royal Tank Regiment

Harry Tresidder was born in Fulledge, near the town of Burnley in Lancashire. After leaving school, he took up a job as a farm labourer. When the war started, Harry joined the Home Guard.

In 1942, Harry tried for the first time for enlistment in the Army on 9 February 1942, but was refused. Not giving up, he tried again on 12 March 1942 and was accepted. He enlisted at Southampton.

After basic military training, he was selected for special training as a Gunner Mechanic on tanks. He also passed a wireless operator course on 5 June 1943.

Gunner Harry Tresidder sitting on left tank track.

Harry was posted to North Africa with the Royal Tank Regiment and served in the desert including the Battle of El Alamein. He was awarded the Africa Star and the 8th Army Clasp. Harry left the Army on 29 March 1946.

Harry's wife, Phyllis, was born in London. She lived with her grandparents and later moved to Bolham in Devon when she was five years old, attending Bolham School.

She moved to Tiverton and attended the "Tiverton Girls' School". Phyllis left school at fourteen and worked for Lady Heathcote Amory in Bolham House.

When the war started, Phyllis, for her war effort, worked in the Tiverton silk factory, making parachutes. She described the different materials and colours of the parachutes. Land droppers were made of white or khaki silk. The supply droppers were made of cotton, and there were different colours for various supplies – for example, ammunition, food or clothing – making it easier for the receiving troops on the ground to identify them.

Harry Tresidder's medal award list.

Phyllis worked at the silk factory for the duration of the war, working up to twelve hours a day.

After the war, Phyllis and her parents moved to Windmill Farm, Montacute and she got a job at Abbot-Clothier, making gloves. She used to cycle to work.

While at Windmill, Phyllis met Harry, her future husband; Harry worked on the farm. Love blossomed and they eventually married in 1947. In later years they had two sons and a daughter, moved to Montacute Prefabs and eventually to Park View, Montacute.

Kenneth Trotman
Royal Air Force Regiment

Ken is on the left but the other two are unknown to the Author.

Ken was raised in Stoke-sub-Hamdon, living at New Road and was called for service to the armed forces in 1940 at the age of twenty years. He joined the Royal Air Force Regiment, attended his medical at York, was declared fit for service and posted to Penzance, Cornwall. Later he was posted to Cardiff and Bridgnorth. Ken also spent a time at Lichfield where he was offered promotion but declined it.

In 1941 Ken was posted to Duxford Airfield, Cambridgeshire and he remembers spending his twenty-first birthday in a gun position for airfield defence in very bad weather.

It was at this particular airfield, that fighter command (12 Group) was stationed. From here, Douglas Bader led 242 Squadron during the Battle of Britain. Together with other squadrons these were known as the Duxford Wing. Their prime role was to protect the Midlands from German attacks but when necessary would be called upon to help 11 Group in the south. On one occasion, while Ken was on airfield defence, he witnessed a JU88 German bomber landing to surrender itself.

Eventually Ken was ordered overseas. He was not told of his destination or anything about it; he boarded a ship on the Clyde and sailed at night to Gibraltar.

On passage into the Mediterranean Ken remembers the ship's engines being silenced as a warning came through of German U boats operating in their vicinity. The ship continued with a zigzag course to avoid detection by any further U boats and sailed through the Suez Canal. Ken remembers leaning over the side of the ship watching camel trains being led along the banks of the canal.

By this time they knew they were destined for Bombay, India. The Regiment left the ship and went to the south of Burma, living in bamboo huts and acting as a reserve force for the Army in the event of an invasion.

With the war ending in the Far East, Ken returned to England and eventually to his home in Montacute.

Corporal Norman Tulett
1156579
Royal Air Force

Norman Tulett was born on 10 June 1922 at Walderton, West Sussex, but moved and went to school in the village of Albury in Surrey. He left school at fourteen and trained to become a mechanic in a garage.

On 3 September 1939, Norman volunteered to join the Royal Air Force. After a medical on 3 June 1940, he reported to Cardington to sign on for the RAF and travelled to Wednesford for basic training, followed by a Flight Mechanics' course.

Corporal Norman Tulett (top right).

He remembers being on guard duty at night armed only with a broom handle with instructions to report to the guard room in case of a disturbance. While stationed here he recalls the night bombing raids of 13 – 17 August on Birmingham. He spent his weekend leave in the Nuffield Club.

After some home leave, he was posted to Middle Wallop in Hampshire, to 604 Squadron, Night Fighters. The aircraft were short nosed Blenheims and Beaufighters. The Commanding Officer was Wing Commander John Cunningham, nicknamed "Cats' Eyes Cunningham". Norman describes Wing Commander Cunningham as a "proper gentleman" who would help his crew as much as possible.

Norman said that while he was at Middle Wallop it was very cold and before operations he had to help de-ice the entire surface area of the aircraft before flying. Norman remarks on the procedure to prime the engine for engine starts on the Beaufighter This was done under the engine, outside, not in the cockpit, before the pilot switched on the ignition to fire up the engines.

He remembers his pilot's name was Sergeant Peter Jackson but could not remember the wireless operator, or the air crewman who operated the equipment for detecting enemy aircraft when airborne who also reloaded the guns as required.

Norman was at Middle Wallop from 1 October to 27 December 1940. After Middle Wallop, Norman was posted to Insworth on 27 December for training as an engine fitter. The course should have been twelve weeks but owing to a shortage of fitters, it had to be completed in nine.

In 1941, Norman was posted to the Middle East. He sailed on the troopship, *Strathnaver*, leaving the Clyde in Scotland and sailing as part of a convoy of twenty five ships. They called in at Freetown on the Gold Coast of Africa. He described the crossing as dreadful with people being sea sick, and mountainous waves.

The next part of the voyage took Norman to the opposite coastline, calling at Port Tufic and then by train to Abu Ker, west of Alexandria, to a transit camp. Here the inmates of the camp had to take cover at night to protect themselves against German aircraft strafing the camp with machine gun fire.

Norman's job was to assist the refuelling of fighter aircraft, Hurricanes and Spitfires, which arrived on an emergency landing strip created in the bush country.

This was all done using 'jerry' cans with the petrol strained through a chamois leather to eliminate dust and sand. They were assisted by the local natives. The aircraft were travelling from the Gold Coast to the Sudan. Later, Norman was posted to Luxor and went from Wadi Halfa by train, to help with the evacuation of Crete, transporting personnel back by flying boat to Luxor in the Nubian Desert.

Norman and some of his fellow airmen volunteered for aircrew but on being told there was a long waiting list, relinquished the idea. He was, for a while, at the Malakal landing strip which he said was infested with snakes; they were everywhere.

In 1942, Norman went to Tobruk in North Africa and then flew out to Biskra in Southern Algiers in the Sahara Desert, working at a maintenance unit where aircraft were sent for servicing. He then moved to Maison Blanche, the main aircraft maintenance unit in Algiers. He remembers seeing General de Gaulle on many occasions.

In Algiers Norman witnessed a Dakota aircraft on fire over an airfield. The propeller fell off and then the engine came away from its casing and sadly the aircraft crashed. While here he also saw a crash site and wreckage of a Westland Lysander which he photographed...

Westland Lysander crash.

Once, when servicing a York four-engined transport aircraft, Norman was standing on the wing of the aircraft when suddenly a propeller from one of the engines started turning. He hastily got off the wing and hurried to get inside the aeroplane. He made his way to the cockpit and found an airman trying to start the engines. Norman hurriedly switched off the fuel cocks and demanded of the operative, "What on earth are you doing, are you trying to kill me?"

Norman also said the airman had his hand on the under carriage lever. If he had pulled this, the aircraft would have dropped to the ground and may have suffered severe damage Norman said that the airman had not been trained to carry out these duties.

Norman was posted to Rabat, Morocco. After Rabat, he returned to Algiers for a forty-eight hour pass to Casablanca and then left on a ship for the United Kingdom. Landing in the Clyde, Norman got his disembarkation leave and went to Blackpool.

After leave, his next posting was Docking in Norfolk, an Air Sea Rescue squadron operating twin-engined Warwicks. These aircraft would carry a twin engined lifeboat, designed by the yachtsman Uffa Fox, to be dropped by parachute from 700ft as near as possible to the downed aircrews to aid their recovery.

Corporal Norman Tulett was released from the RAF on 23rd April 1946.

Amy Bugler (née Wall)
Land Army 1944-45

Amy pictured at ninety-two years with her Land Army medal and citation.

Amy was born in 1922 near Wedmore, Somerset, and attended school at Chapel Allerton. When she was eleven years old, she went to Wedmore School and leaving school at fourteen became nanny to a child living in Blackford, Somerset.

When Amy was eighteen, she joined the Land Army and worked on a farm owned by a Mr Colmer, at Blackford. Amy started work at 6.30 a.m. milking cows, feeding calves and other stock and general farm work till six at night, an approximately twelve hour day, seven days a week.

Later, Amy went to work on her uncle's farm, Farmer Kelly at Powerstock near Bridport – doing the same type of work. She stayed there for about twelve months and when she met her husband, Bob Bugler, was married in Chapel Allerton and returned to live in Powerstock, Dorset, where she worked on the land together with Bob until 1945.

Amy and Bob moved back to Somerset in 1945 and bought a house at Percombe Hill near Stoke sub Hamdon; Bob drove a cattle lorry for Mr Cornelius. They stayed at Percombe for ten years before moving to Foldhill Lane, near Ash, Somerset, where she remembers feeding some sheep in the bad winter of 1963.

After a while, they moved to East Lambrook and lived there for twenty-five years, eventually moving to Montacute in 1991.

Two years ago, Amy was presented with her Land Army medal and citation, signed by David Cameron, the Prime Minister, which she is very proud of. Amy is now ninety-two but still very active in mind and body.

Major Edward Warrick
Royal Engineers

Born in 1924, one of three brothers and a sister, Edward Warrick lived in London until war came in September 1939. All Edward's brothers, and his sister, joined the Armed Forces.

In 1939, when Ted was fourteen years old, he went to live in Sevenoaks, Kent. In June 1940, with the Germans advancing through France, the family could hear the sound of heavy artillery from across the Channel. Ted also remembers, during the evacuation of Dunkirk, seeing wounded soldiers on trains passing through Sevenoaks.

Realising the danger of a possible invasion, Edward and his mother decided to move to the country. Loading up the car with their possessions, including two shotguns, they proceeded on their journey, map reading all the way because of the lack of signposts which had been taken away so as not to aid the enemy forces. Edward and his mother eventually arrived at Curry Mallet in Somerset and rented a farmhouse for three months.

Edward reflected that these were exciting times for a schoolboy, living in the country in war time with a lot to explore. He remembers cycling around the countryside watching with interest the building of pillboxes and

Edward Warrick in Home Guard
uniform 1940.

Edward Warrick in desert kit 1943.

tank traps, also the construction of airfields and barrage balloon sites.

After a few weeks' holiday in the countryside, Edward was sent to Cheltenham School in September 1940. Here he joined the school cadet force, and later joined the Gloucester Home Guard. He was surprised to find out later that this qualified him for the Defence Medal and the Victory Medal.

In 1943, he left school and joined the Royal Engineers, training at Aldershot, where he was promoted to Lieutenant. Edward was posted to Arabia, with further postings to Cyprus and eventually Palestine, assisting the peace keeping forces.

Lieutenant Warrick remained in the Army after the war and retired with the rank of Major.

Reginald John Wilton
5671917 7th Battalion
Somerset Light Infantry

Reginald Wilton was born in Glamorgan, Wales in 1919, but the family traces back to Somerset. Reg's father heralded from Yeovil being born in 1879. His name was William Wilton and he lived at Bishopston, Montacute in 1891 and worked as a general labourer in the villages of Montacute, Martock and South Petherton.

In 1911 Reg's father, seeking work, travelled to Wales and worked as a miner; here he lodged with a family from Stoke sub Hamdon by the name of Shoemark.

In 1915 Reg's father met Elizabeth Poole and they were married at Wellington, Somerset.

Eventually the Wiltons returned to Montacute and when the Second World War came, Reginald joined the 7th Battalion Somerset Light Infantry. The Somersets fought their way, after landing in Normandy, to the River Elbe. The Somersets were described as the finest fighting men to go up against the German army.

It was during these battles that Reginald John Wilton was killed in action on the 9 August 1944 aged twenty-five years and was laid to rest with honours at St Manvieu War Cemetery, Cheux, France.

Amy Yates LDG WREN (W.R.N.S.)
31.3.1943 – 24.8.46

Amy joined the WRNS on 31 March 1943 at HMS *Drake*, Plymouth and became a writer in the WRNS office at Royal Naval Engineering College, Devonport. In the next year she watched the preparations for "D Day" including the involvement of the Americans.

In 1944 Amy applied for overseas service and this was granted in August of that year. She found herself among 200 WRNS and 200 RAF chaps onboard the liner *Stratheden* en route for Bombay and Colombo.

The ship sailed down through the Atlantic and into the Mediterranean calling at Port Said, Egypt and the troops were allowed to buy fruit,

chocolate, and Turkish Delight, but after these had been taken on board, the ship became infested with ants being attracted by the sweets. As the weather became more tropical, anyone who could sew was in much demand to make the khaki shorts even shorter!

The voyage took the ship through the Suez Canal and on to Aden and then Bombay. Here the WRNS changed ship to the SS *Nevassa* and for those few moments Amy did set foot in India. Finally Amy arrived at Colombo taking up her duties working in the Main Drafting Office where all the Naval records were kept on a card index system. She describes it as "much better and more accurate than the computers of today!"

In July 1945 she was on the move again – this time to Mombasa, Kenya, to HMS *Tana*, a shore establishment. This time the ship involved was even smaller, the SS *Hunan*, which before the war had plied its way up and down the Yangtze River in China. The ship belonged to the Chinese Navigation Company and, escaping from the Japanese, had made its way to the Indian ocean to transport people and stores around. During the voyage to Mombasa the ship docked at Port Victoria in the Seychelles. Amy had a day ashore – "the islands were quite undeveloped then", Amy says. Back at sea they heard the news about the dropping of the atomic bomb on Hiroshima. Amy said, "it was obvious the war would soon be over."

Arriving in Mombasa she resumed her duties as a writer in the WRNS office. The WRNS quarters housed approximately 1000 WRNS. Mombasa was very peaceful. Amy described cycling with a friend round the streets of Kilindini unescorted during her off duty hours, spending time on the golf course and watching the Dhows sailing up and down past Fort Jesus.

Eventually Amy returned home to England via Naples (to off-load Italian prisoners of war) and finally sailed up the Clyde passing the two great ships the *Queen Mary* and *Queen Elizabeth*.

On 24 August 1946 Amy was demobbed with a clothes gratuity of £12.10s.0d.

VICTORY CELEBRATIONS

When the war ended in Europe in May 1945 and in the Far East in August 1945, it was welcome news in Great Britain and world-wide.

It was a huge relief for families in cities, towns and villages not to have to make any more sacrifices in the cause of freedom. It gave the village of Montacute great pride in the following months to welcome back the service men and women after their years overseas, serving King and country.

On V.E. Day, the village celebrated the end of war in Europe with bonfires. Shirley Hann remembers a huge bonfire on Ladies' Walk Hill, and instead of fireworks, which were forbidden, parishioners somehow obtained rook scarers (a very loud banger) which created even more noise.

Ivan Chick recalls another bonfire on St Michael's Hill.

I have no recollection of street parties in the village but expect this kind of activity would have been limited because of food rationing, but individual families would have celebrated their loved ones returning to their own homes. [Author]

8th June, 1946

TO-DAY, AS WE CELEBRATE VICTORY.

I send this personal message to you and all other boys and girls at school. For you have shared in the hardships and dangers of a total war and you have shared no less in the triumph of the Allied Nations.

I know you will always feel proud to belong to a country which was capable of such supreme effort; proud, too, of parents and elder brothers and sisters who by their courage, endurance and enterprise brought victory. May these qualities be yours as you grow up and join in the common effort to establish among the nations of the world unity and peace.

George R.I.

King George VI
Victory message.

INDEX